Boxing Like the Champs

Lessons from Boxing's Greatest Fighters

Mark Hatmaker

Jack Dempsey

Tracks Publishing
Ventura, California

Boxing Like the Champs
Lessons from Boxing's Greatest Fighters
Mark Hatmaker

Tracks Publishing
458 Dorothy Avenue
Ventura, CA 93003
1-805-754-0248
tracks@cox.net
www.startupsports.com
trackspublishing.com

Copyright © 2016 by Mark Hatmaker and Doug Werner
10 9 8 7 6 5 4 3 2

Publisher's Cataloging-in-Publication

Names:
Hatmaker, Mark, author.

Title:
Boxing like the champs : lessons from boxing's greatest fighters / Mark Hatmaker.

Description:
San Diego, California : Tracks Publishing, [2016] I Meant to be used in an interlocking synergistic manner with the author's other boxing mastery manuals.-- Page 7. I Includes bibliographical references and index.

Identifiers:
ISBN: 978-1-935937-76-0 I LCCN: 2016941689

Subjects:
LCSH: Boxing. I Boxing--History. I Boxing--Psychological aspects. I Boxers (Sports)--Training. I Boxers (Sports)--Training--History. I Boxers (Sports)--Psychological aspects. I Boxers (Sports)--Biography. I BISAC: SPORTS & RECREATION / Boxing.

Classification:
LCC: GV1137.6 .H385 2016 I DDC: 796.83--dc23

Books by Mark Hatmaker

No Holds Barred Fighting:
The Ultimate Guide to Submission Wrestling

More No Holds Barred Fighting:
Killer Submissions

No Holds Barred Fighting:
Savage Strikes

No Holds Barred Fighting:
Takedowns

No Holds Barred Fighting:
The Clinch

No Holds Barred Fighting:
The Ultimate Guide to Conditioning

No Holds Barred Fighting:
The Kicking Bible

No Holds Barred Fighting:
The Book of Essential Submissions

Boxing Mastery

No Second Chance:
A Reality-Based Guide to Self-Defense

MMA Mastery:
Flow Chain Drilling and Integrated O/D Training

MMA Mastery:
Ground and Pound

MMA Mastery:
Strike Combinations

Boxer's Book of Conditioning & Drilling

Boxer's Bible of Counterpunching

Mud, Guts & Glory
Tips & Training for Extreme Obstacle Racing

She's Tough
Extreme Fitness Training for Women

Boxing for MMA

*Books are available through major bookstores
and booksellers on the Internet.*

Dedicated to the human fist and
all the beautiful and magnificent
destruction it can do when
wielded by two gritty and gracious
sportsmen.

This book would not have been
possible without Kylie Hatmaker
and Shane Tucker.

Edited by Phyllis Carter

Contents

Mike and Tommy Gibbons

How to use the Boxing Mastery Manuals

This book and the others in this series are meant to be used in an interlocking, synergistic manner where the sum value of the manuals is greater than the individual parts. What we are striving to do with each manual is to focus on a specific aspect of the sport and give thoughtful consideration to the necessary ideas, tactics and strategies pertinent to the facet of focus. We are aware that this piecemeal approach may seem lacking if one only consumes one or two manuals at most, but we are confident that once three or more manuals have been studied, the overall picture or method will begin to reveal itself.

Since the manuals are interlocking there is no single manual in the series that is meant to be complete in and of itself. They are all made stronger by an understanding of the material that preceded it. And so on and so forth with each manual in this series. Now, let's lace up those gloves!

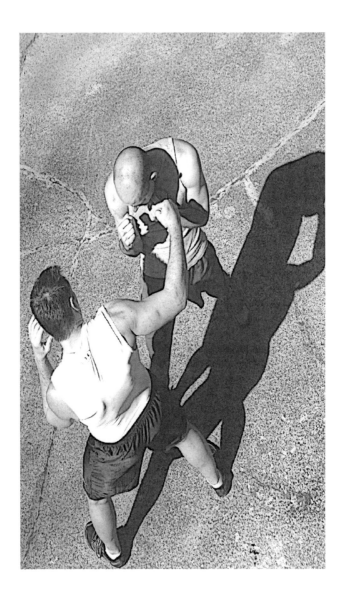

Brains and fists

Hello Reader!

Let's start things off right with doing something rather than just reading. Hold up your hand. Seriously, I want you to do it right now.

> Brains and fists working together as one solid team — that's what this book is all about.

Look at it. Now make a fist. Turn it this way and that as you peer at it from all aspects.

Your clenched fist, whether wielding a weapon or being a weapon itself, has always been the great equalizer in this world. We lack the brawn and brute strength of the silverback gorilla; we walk nakedly without prominent fangs and razor sharp claws; we have no thick protective hide; no cheetah-like speed; no astounding leaps and bounds to escape like the springbok and other such nimble species. We have no rack of impressive antlers to butt with; no horns to hook with; quills or scent to deter with; no naturally secreted venom to strike and inject with.

Look at that fist. This, for the most part, is what we have used to claw our way to the top of the heap — the clenched human fist along with the human brain to think up all sorts of ways to use it. Brains and fists working together as one solid team — that's what this book is all about.

Anyone can close their hand and sling it at someone. They may even do some damage if they are much larger or catch their quarry off guard. But once you put a thinking, calculating brain inside that fist-wielder, you encounter an entirely different animal. One that is also capable of destruction and, oddly enough since we are speaking of doing violence, beauty.

Human beings admire power and a job well done. Masterly fisticuffs can often times rise to the level of science and even poetry. Your fist is essentially no different from any other fist on the planet so in theory we should be able to be as awe inspiring as our weight class allows.

What separates your fist, my fist and most fists from true legendary status is the brain and intention behind it. That and lots and lots of practice. This manual is going to take an inside look at some of the past greats to see if we can shine a light on how these undisputed masters of fistic science did what they did with this common tool.

Let's look at that fist one more time: Twenty-seven bones bonded by sheaths of muscle, tendon, ligament and skin guided by one human brain. We can't change our fists and what comprises them, but we can put new information into our brains to better use those 27 bones. Let's do that with some of the best fistic minds that ever walked the planet.

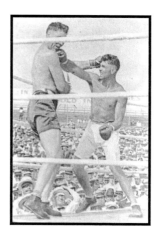

1. Building a fist like Jack Dempsey

Let's start our first lesson with what should be a given by now — building a fist. But before we do that, let's talk tough. Tough with a capital T — Jack Dempsey Tough.

How tough is Jack Dempsey Tough?

He racked up a tally of 50 knockouts in 81 bouts. If we add his exhibition bouts, the win tally becomes well-nigh uncountable and that KO record goes up as well. The renowned boxing historian Bert Randolph Sugar discovered a truly astonishing Dempsey knockout total. According to Mr. Sugar, Dempsey scored 60 knockouts in the first round alone. Yeah, I'd call that tough.

On September 14, 1923, Jack Dempsey fought Luis Angel Firpo, "El Toro de las Pampas" or The Bull of the Pampas. Firpo was the bigger man at 227 pounds. The Champ weighed in at 192. The opening round is legend. Almost immediately Firpo caught Jack with a right that dropped him to his knee. He recovered, swarmed El Toro and dropped him not once, not twice, not thrice, but a total of seven times in that first round (no three-knockdown rule to get in Jack's way back then).

Just when ringsiders thought it couldn't get any wilder, El Toro caught Dempsey with a good right hand. Jack does not hit the canvas, but goes through the ropes and completely out of the ring. We are talking big fall here — an ass-over-head dive. Dempsey crashed and cut the back of his head on a sportswriter's typewriter (or "writing machine" in some accounts.) The referee started the count while sportswriters scrambled to get Jack back into the ring. The count hit four and the battle raged on. Round two was relatively mild in comparison — Dempsey dropped El Toro twice before Firpo simply could not get up.

Jack Dempsey was a tough, relentless fighter who knew how to maximize his power. But that power had to be delivered through his fists, and he felt that there was a bit of science that goes into building that fist. Notice, I said building the fist and not making a fist. A fist to Dempsey was something to be engineered and not a mere clinching of the fingers.

A note from the Deep South

You will notice in these photos that I box southpaw. I'm a natural righty who retrained southpaw to put coordinated/power-side forward and to beef up my "weak" hand. In other words, I sincerely see power-side forward as not losing a power hand, but putting power into both hands.

Nowhere in these pages will you find me preaching to you to make the switch. I just bring up my obvious southpaw stance for the question that usually follows: "I'm an orthodox fighter, will this book work for me?" Yep. No worries, boxing is boxing. Southpaws, follow my lead, literally. Orthodox fighters, flip the photos in your mind and we're all on the same page.

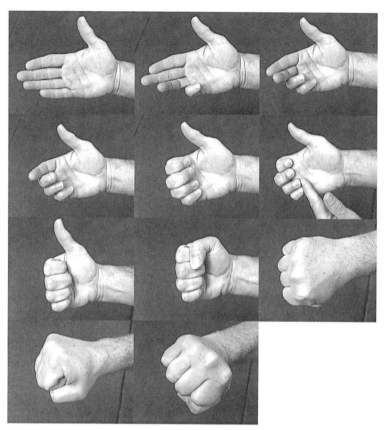

Engineering the Dempsey fist

● With your hand open wide, begin curling the fingers into the upper portion of your palm.

● You'll want to curl the little finger first, followed by the ring finger, then middle and, finally, the index finger.

● It is vital that you "pack" the fist tight by tucking the fingertips as close to the base of the fingers as you can manage.

● Finally, fold the thumb over the curled knuckles of the index and middle fingers.

Think that's all there is to it? Not hardly.

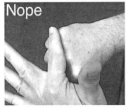
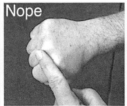
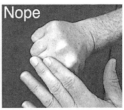

Striking surface

Mr. Dempsey was very particular about the striking surface of the fist. There are some who will tell you to strike with the top face of the knuckles, or the prominent knuckles of the index and middle fingers or the flat of the index and middle fingers.

The champ would say that the correct striking surface is the flat surface of the bottom three fingers — the little, ring and middle fingers. The Champ found that this striking surface seemed to line up naturally with skeletal support from the radius and ulna of the forearm, creating in essence one fused piece of bone from shoulder to striking surface. He felt that all other striking surface variations called for a bit of adjustment in the wrist to make the striking surface "work." And that making it work often led to injuring the wrist or the fist itself.

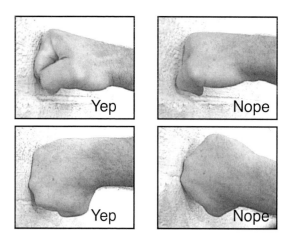

Yep · Nope · Yep · Nope

Wall test

There's a simple way to test the stability of the Champ's built fist and the other variations. Stand in front of a wall and build your fist. Place the tested striking surface against the wall and push HARD. Don't punch, just push. Run this test through each of the striking surfaces mentioned. You will feel for yourself that the Champ's fist is the only one that naturally lines up with no need of tweak to correct alignment that could lead to injury down the road.

Jack Dempsey was a powerful puncher. He felt that a hard puncher needed a good weapon to punch with, and his built fist was that weapon.

Crafty tactics from the Champs

The next several lessons will allow us to adopt and adapt powerful and crafty tactics from some of the best fighters to have ever stepped into the ring.

2. Little Chocolate and the clinch jab

George Dixon, aka "Little Chocolate," was one of the scrappiest bantam and featherweights the early era produced. Often tipping the scales at no more than 87 pounds, Dixon began his boxing career almost exclusively as a left-handed fighter. He had the speed, the evasive footwork and the gas in the tank to keep him out of harm's way while not seeming to look for the knockout. And by gas in the tank, I'm talking world-class stamina. He engaged in many long battles, one of which was a 70-round draw versus the "American" bantamweight title holder, Cal McCarthy. Dixon might have coasted along on his left-handed laurels just fine, but he was fortunate enough to come under the tutelage of manager Tom O'Rourke.

O'Rourke was a crafty welterweight at one time and recognized the natural ability in Dixon, but saw that the fighter would need to develop a right hand to go further. With that in mind, he set out working almost exclusively on Dixon's right, developing stiff straight arms and chopping hooks to the body.

In this lesson I want to focus on what Dixon started doing with his left hand once he found his right. Pre-O'Rourke, Dixon had, according to all accounts, a very quick left jab. Once Dixon became confident with his right hand he used his left less and opted to find ways to do maximum damage

> He engaged in many long battles, one of which was a 70-round draw ...

with only his right.

Yes, he would still use his left, but it was primarily to get to a head clinch where he would then go to work with stiff rights to the head and hooks to the body while keeping the head under control. Often the way Dixon would apply punching inside the clinch blurred the lines in the boxing rule set, but it is perfectly legal inside MMA.

What we'll do here is show how Dixon used his jab as a clinch jab and show drills for hitting while holding, and the definitely kosher version of using the clinch jab to get to an overhook clinch.

The clinch jab is a surprisingly crafty tool well worth working on. A sneaky tactic conjured in the mind of the man whose tombstone reads:

THE GAMEST PUGILIST THAT EVER LIVED

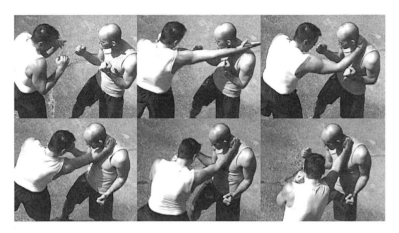

Clinch jab

● Throw a jab almost as if you were throwing a loose, open lead hook. The object is less to strike with the punch than to allow the hand to pass to the side of the head where it can then grip the back of the head or neck with the palm of the punching hand.

● Immediately drive the clinching elbow across your opponent's chest and into him while maintaining your head clinch.

● At the same time, slide step toward your clinch-hand side. Doing these motions in concert causes your opponent to step forward with his far foot and essentially step into your rear-hand punch. Drill the clinch jab in isolation until setting it with the hand and elbow together with the footwork feels crisp.

Now let's get offensive with this tool.

Clinch jab to rear straight

● Hook the clinch jab, then fire a rear straight hand to the face.

Clinch jab to body hook

● Hook the clinch jab then fire a rear hook to the body.
● Feel free to double up the two rear hands into combinations. Dixon did so often, firing multiple right hands while maintaining head control.

Wheeling out

Once you have finished your inside attack and it's time to disengage, you can't simply step out since this leaves you open to counter. Instead...

● Place the rear hand on his far shoulder or far biceps.
● Push him away with both hands in their anchor position as you pivot on your lead foot away from him.

Clinch jab to biceps ride

● Use Dixon's clinch jab to control with a loose open clinch.
● Hook your clinch jab.
● With the rear hand ride/muffle the far biceps or shoulder.
● If you keep steady across-and-in pressure with the head-clinch elbow, you have a surprising amount of control.
● Use the wheel-out when it is time to leave or …

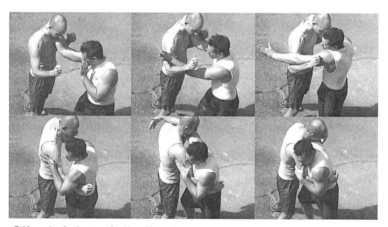

Clinch jab to full clinch

● Hook a clinch jab and follow with the preceding biceps ride.
● Step into your opponent and hook, sliding first the biceps ride to an overhook clinch and then sliding the head-control hand down to an overhook.
● *Note:* With the head-control hand, don't simply take your hand off the head and hook the overhook. This leaves an arm unmonitored and you will be open for body shots.
● Instead, as you release the head, slide the elbow down along the inside of your opponent's arm until you reach the bottom of the biceps and then shoot the overhook.

3. Johnny Dundee and the leaping hook

Johnny Dundee, with his now politically incorrect ring name, "The Scotch Wop," was one of the busiest fighters of the early 20th century. This featherweight and junior lightweight titleholder fought more rounds in his ring career than any other champion — 335 — with only 31 losses. Dundee also

shares the dubious distinction of having one of the all-time lowest knockout rates at seven percent. Some call him out on this, but Dundee saw it as part and parcel of his style.

Dundee was a fast man with a speedy, yet powerless punch. Boxing has a long history of speedy men in the lighter weight divisions, but one thing that sets Dundee apart is his incessant, almost kangarooish in-and-out footwork style. Dundee was noted for his "be there and then be gone" way of punching, often leaping in with his lead hook without bothering to set his feet for the punch. He would dart in and out — leaping and shifting almost incessantly.

Many boxers with an in-and-out style adopt more of a fencing approach where you use sliding foot work to advance deeply and fire punches and then slide out of harm's way. Nothing so staid for Dundee. He would bounce on his toes with boundless energy, whether he was in range or not

In films he often looks to be performing a long, showboating dance with lunging advances and retreats so powerful he would at times ricochet off the ropes on the exit.

To adopt Dundee's style you've got to have confidence in your conditioning. But even if you don't adopt it wholeheartedly, there is something to be learned from his leaping hook.

Leaping hook footwork
● Push forward aggressively with the rear foot and leap onto the lead foot approximately 18 inches in front of you.
● As soon as your lead foot lands, followed rapidly by the rear foot sliding up, fire off the lead foot and immediately leap 18 inches in retreat.

It is recommended that you work this footwork without the hook for a few rounds to get used to the rabbity nature of the movement. It will indeed feel unnatural at first.

Leaping hook

● To add the leaping hook to the mix, you want to time a loose lead hook to connect with the chin exactly at the moment the lead foot hits the canvas.

● Do not set looking for a second punch, execute the retreating leap immediately.

To be sure, there is little stink or power on this leaping hook, but the strategic element of surprise you can gain by having the ability to gambit such a long range, in-and-out tool is well worth the practice. Big thanks to Mr. Johnny Dundee.

4. Jose Napoles and his hot buttery lead hand

Cuban-born emigre to Mexico Jose Napoles was a mighty smooth welterweight champion. He would often assume a quasi-crouch and with subtle bobs and weaves sting with either hand. Both were things of beauty, but it was the facile use of that lead hand that earned him the name "Mantequilla" which in Spanish means butter. This lead hand was so smooth it was indeed buttery, and he found so many ways to use it, a better name might have been "Cuchillo Caliente" or "hot knife" because that lead hand performed like a hot knife through butter.

Napoles had an artful ability to make that jab work like a hammering piston. He would throw doubles and triples with regularity, but where many fighters who double and triple up on the jab appear to be flicking after the first jab, each of Mantequilla's jabs looked as solid as the first. He also used the lead hand to hook off the jab, and again this was no token offering of the jab to get to the lead hook. He threw all of these multiples with seamless, equalized precision.

Often waiting behind his left hand work would be a powerful right — a straight rear hand in most vocabularies, but Napoles favored the rear uppercut. He'd get his man worried about the straight jabs and the outside line and then that rear uppercut would come up the middle and do its business.

Boxing coaches from time immemorial and round the world will tell you combinations are where it's at — punches in bunches — but seldom do you find such bunching used so consistently well in a single hand.

With this single-handed agility in mind, let's see what we can do about making our lead hand a little more buttery.

Double jab

● We all know what needs to be done here, but to throw it like Napoles, we must execute a complete rechambering before firing again. No half measures — merely vibrating the fist at the end of a punch.

● Work on firing the double and then moving offline immediately.

Triple jab

● You know what to do.

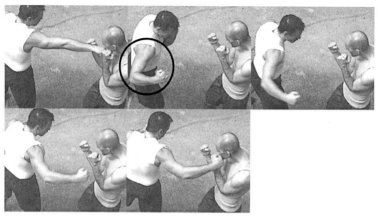

Hook off the jab

● Fire a jab and rechamber completely.

● While rechambering, start cheating the lead shoulder a little to the outside (as shown above) so that the hook is preloaded for firing. The sequence below shows the standard rechambering.

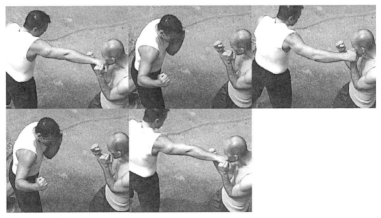

Jab-hook-jab

This is another slick combo from Mantequilla.

● Execute the hook off the jab from the prior drill.

● Remember to rechamber by cheating the lead shoulder a little to the outside like before.

● Fire another jab.

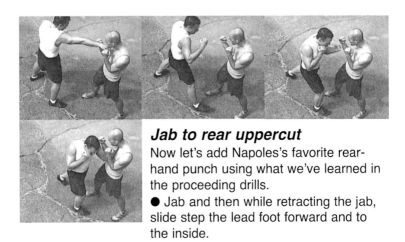

Jab to rear uppercut

Now let's add Napoles's favorite rear-hand punch using what we've learned in the proceeding drills.

● Jab and then while retracting the jab, slide step the lead foot forward and to the inside.

● Once inside, immediately fire a rear uppercut.

Repeat the preceding with:

Double jab to rear uppercut

Triple jab to rear uppercut

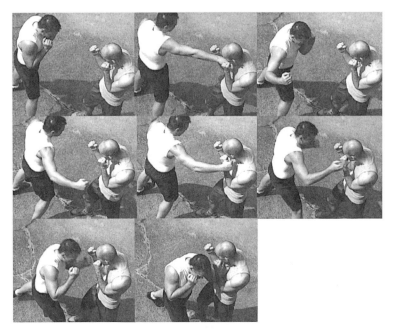

Hook off the jab to rear uppercut

If you work through these drills with diligence, you just may transform your own lead hand from bland, fake margarine to rich, creamy butter.

5. Artistry of Eder Jofre

Bantamweight and featherweight champion Eder Jofre of Brazil was born to be a warrior. His family on both his mother's and his father's side was deeply populated with boxers and wrestlers. One uncle was a European middleweight champ, another uncle held the Brazilian lightweight title, and his father was a skilled lightweight who fought under the name Kid Jofre. Even the distaff side of the family was imbued with the combat sprit — an aunt was one of Argentina's top female wrestlers.

Indeed Eder seemed destined to follow familiar footsteps, and he did so in a big way. Practically raised in his father's gym, he was throwing his hands with speed and authority from an early age. His skills earned him a spot in the 1956 Olympics as a bantamweight where he lost in the quarter final to an opponent he would later knockout as a pro, Claudio Barrientos.

Eder had speed, power and defense — there is much to learn from this boxer. Let's hone in on a few eccentricities in his style that at first glance appear to be bad form, but upon closer inspection and with a little experimentation, we realize these "mistakes" were made on purpose to maximize speed and power.

Jofre lesson #1: Tip jab

Eder would often jab from the outside where we see him lean forward and come up high on the rear toes. Usually an ungrounded punch like this has little authority and yet when it lands we see the sweat snap off his opponents. Eder was not tipping his jab as a mere flick, he was timing the entire body for power.

Tip jab

● As you jab from the outside, stand tall and allow your rear toes to drive off of the ground to full extension.

● When we freeze the tip jab at the end point, we see the entire body in one long line tipped forward toward your target with the toes of the rear foot just barely in contact with the canvas.

● We must time the end of our jab's extension with the moment the body goes "long" and the toes reach full extension.

● Once we coordinate these motions, this bit of "bad form" transforms into a tool of authority. I find that the tip jab is tough to drill or learn in shadow or mirror work because we will feel off balance at the end of the punch when inertia draws us forward. But once we take this coordinated movement to the heavy bag or pads and find the timing of the concerted movement, you will find your "Aha!" moment.

Jofre lesson #2: Cross-step jab

Boxing coaches will tell you not to cross your feet while moving. Hell, it's not even wise to bring your feet closer than a foot apart. Damn good advice that was broken on a regular basis by Jofre. He was constantly crossing the rear foot outside and behind the lead foot as he fired a jab and moved out of the way.

If we pay close attention, we realize that this was not a tactical error or a simple "bother" jab. As he moved defensively, he was using his footwork in a coordinated way to put some stink on a jab that a simple slide step to the outside often does not provide. This one is subtle, so let's break it down.

Cross-step jab

● Picture firing a jab as you make the "mistake" of stepping the rear foot behind and past the lead foot.

● You will want to time the jab to land as the rear foot makes the swing past the foot.

Now pay close attention as this is where the magic is. We know that standard jabs (and all punches for that matter) are powered by a good hip or waist twist to put more mass behind the punch.

What Jofre is doing is not merely stepping "poorly." He is swinging his rear leg around and behind with intent. He is in essence using the rear leg as a pendulum that snaps or rotates the hips giving authority to the jab. This aggressive pendulum provides the hip-twist force that is usually accomplished while standing on two feet.

● This is one that you can feel with shadow and mirror work. I advise you to drill until you find your timing.
● Then take it to the heavy bag and pads. Once you find the right pendulum pop, you'll wonder why you didn't think of it yourself.

Jofre Lesson #3: Leaping outside jab

Jofre often would use the preceding tactic in concert with a little hop. It has the appearance of a devil-may-care show-boat move, but once we understand the mechanics of the cross-step jab, we realize that Jofre was leaping or hopping to add additional pop on his pendulum leg swing.

Leaping outside jab

● Perform as you would the cross-step jab except here you will precede with a drive off the rear foot to power the hop to the outside.

● As the lead foot makes contact with the floor after the hop, time the pendulum swing to hip twist the jab into its target.

Jofre Lesson #4: Crunch hook

This is my absolute favorite tip I picked up from the estimable Eder Jofre. Lead hooks are classically thrown, whether cleanly upright or from a crouch, with both feet making a shift to the inside line as you pivot on the balls of both feet to power the hip twist. Jofre would split this pivot in two. He would pivot on the lead foot, but ...

We can see the rear knee advance without the rear foot taking a step or pivoting. Just what is going on here? A bit of brilliance is what. Jofre's rear knee is seen to move not because he is lifting it, but rather because of a cross-abdominal pull that he is using to add power to his hook. Let's break this beauty down.

Crunch hook ━━▶

● As you throw your lead hook, from the very beginning think of doing a cross-abdominal crunch.
● Think of a steel cable attached to the lower rib cage on the jab side of your body with the other end connected to the hip flexor on the opposite side.
● Contract this "cable" aggressively to help fire the hook.
● The rear knee will be seen to lift a little, not because you are actively lifting the knee, but rather as a consequence of the crunch.

I could go all day with Jofre's magic, but these four lessons from this unorthodox master will do for now.

Crunch hook

The sequences at the bottom of the page compare the crunch hook to the traditional lead hook.

6. Frank Erne's two-point feint and long uppercut

Frank Erne was born in Switzerland in 1875, and his parents immigrated to the United States not too long after that. He started boxing at an early age and worked in many gyms of both the boxing and "physical culture" variety. He went on to earn both the featherweight and the lightweight titles.

Erne's knockout record would seem to put him into the lightweight puncher category, but his wins over excellent opponents such as George Dixon, Kid Lavigne and Joe Gans (champions all) show that he could more than hold his own. Let's be clear, Erne would not bristle at being called a lightweight puncher. He avidly pursued finesse and devoted himself to ring generalship to such a degree that many report him as being a boring fighter at times. But this "boring" fighter definitely seemed to know what he was doing. Let's have a look at two of his canny tactics.

Two-point feint

So Erne's methodical nature was not exciting. He would rather conserve energy and throw punches he knew he could land, as opposed to milling and wading in like a Tony Zale, come-hell-or-high-water slugger.

Erne loved the feint or false intention that inspires a defensive reaction that pulls the opponent out of position for the real attack. His go-to move was the two-point feint. He would shoulder feint throwing a jab and if the opponent moved to block the straight left, he would turn the left into a lead hook on this now open line. If the opponent reacted to the feint "one-step ahead" anticipating the hook, Erne would fire his rear straight instead.

It is interesting to note that when using the two-point feint, Erne would seldom fire the actual jab if the opponent defended an anticipated hook. He would usually choose to go with the stronger rear-hand punch.

Shoulder feint

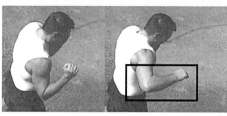

Arm feint

Shoulder and arm feint

● In the mirror, work on refining your shoulder action so that it resembles a jab on the way.

● Start the shoulder forward and get that elbow lifted as if to drive the straight line. When it feels and looks legit, you can take it to the heavy bag or pads.

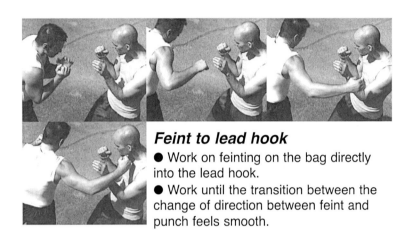

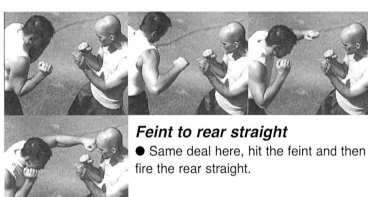

Feint to lead hook
● Work on feinting on the bag directly into the lead hook.
● Work until the transition between the change of direction between feint and punch feels smooth.

Feint to rear straight
● Same deal here, hit the feint and then fire the rear straight.

Ultimately to make these bona fide in the Frank Erne sense, you've got to have a good partner on the pads who will allow you to find and feel the timing and then start mixing it up at random so you can find your feint shift in response to the given defense.

Long uppercut

Another fascinating tactic from Erne is his often used and unusual answer to a long jab — the long uppercut. As the jab was on its way, Erne would often turn his body to the outside to allow the punch to slip over his shoulder. Like most fighters, he would fire his own rear straight in return, but with the hand in an unusual position to create a baffling angle for the defender.

Long uppercut on the bag
● Turn to the outside (your lead shoulder).
● Fire your rear hand, but do not roll the palm downward as you would for a standard rear straight.
● Instead, your palm will split the difference between facing up and inward.
● This unusual fist position allows the fist to travel in an arc that hits a bit more on the button than the standard straight smash to the chin.

Once you've got the hand position down, let's grab a partner with pads since this is a counterfighting move and not meant to be used in isolation.

Long uppercut with partner
● In the midst of your pad set, have your feeder fire a long jab. Slip and counter with a long uppercut.

There are several more tricks in the bag of this "boring" fighter, but these two will whet our appetite until another day.

7. Freddie Welsh's pinpoint jab

The great Freddie Welsh had stamina to burn, but when it came to power, that was another story. Out of a 168-bout career he scored only 32 knockouts. A ringside account of his decision over Willie Ritchie in 1914 to win the lightweight title gives tale to this lack of power, but also allows a glimpse of his boxing mastery. The following is from a ringside reporter's view of the bout.

"[Welsh was able to] bounce three or four thousand light jabs off of the anatomy of Willie Ritchie and dance away. Satisfied to clinch, flop a right to the kidneys, grin, and do it all over again, his punches were harmless as the drop of a butterfly."

Not a terribly inspiring account, unless one reads more into that "three or four thousand jabs" remark, and trust me, there is much to read. Realizing his power deficit, Welsh decided to make up for it with an active (very active) jab. What's more he made a conscious effort to hone it to a dialed in, laser accuracy so that while he could seldom hurt an opponent with one big punch, he could hurt a man by hitting one or two spots hundreds of times.

And that's exactly what he did. Welsh would select tiny, pinpoint targets on an opponent's face or body and zero in on those again and again and again. This repeated punishment would accrue some major results as these unlucky targeted areas would begin to swell with the repeated abuse.

This focused jab attack was not guess work. Welsh honed his jab accuracy by painting a single white dot on the heavy bag and made sure he could hit it unerringly during any move or set of conditions. The following drills will allow us to start developing a bit of that Freddie Welsh pinpoint accuracy.

Freddie Welsh jab drills
Paint a dot on your bag or apply a square of duct tape for your drill target.

Focus drill
● To begin we will simply fire our jab for a few rounds free form, striving to hit the target and nothing but the target.

Sidestep right drill
● Get in front of the bag, fire a quick jab at the target then a fast sidestep to the right.
● As soon as you hit right, fire that jab again.
● Complete as many rounds as necessary for the sidestep jab to be just as accurate as the preliminary jab.

Sidestep left drill
● You know what to do.

Feint to jab drill
● Use any feint you have in your vocabulary, but always come back to fire that jab and hit your mark.
● Feint a lead hook, rear hand, shoulder or feint with the feet — use all the tricks, but always bring it back to that pinpoint jab.

Wheel-out jab

● Fire a preliminary jab on target.
● Envision a rush and wheel the rear foot to the outside and fire another pinpoint jab.

Wheel-in jab

● Fire a preliminary jab.
● Envision a rush, but this time wheel to the inside and fire a pinpoint jab.

Duck-in jab

● Fire the preliminary jab.
● Duck and side step inside and come back up for the pinpoint jab. ● Retreat or wheel out immediately.

Duck-out jab

● Fire a preliminary jab.
● Hit the preceding duck-in jab.
● Duck back down and slide out rising up with a pinpoint jab.

Freeze jab

Welsh was known for his constant motion, so at times he could confuse an opponent by coming to a standstill — dangerous for most fighters. Once he hit that standstill, with zero tell or telegraphing, he'd fire a pinpoint jab and get back on the move.

- To drill a freeze jab, fire a preliminary jab.
- Hit some fast slips and bobs and weaves.
- Freeze, just for a bit, then fire with as little tell as you can.
- *Note:* a mirror is a big help in watching for your tells.

Retreat jab

Welsh was also known for "milling on the retreat." That is, firing while moving backwards. Let's build this version of the pinpoint jab.

● Step in tight to the bag and place your forehead on it.
● Hit a quick slide step to the rear and fire a pinpoint jab.
● It may take a few rounds to find just the right distance on your retreat step to give the jab the room it needs, but it will come with time.

Once you have moved through these incarnations, I highly recommend you taking them to the focus pads so you can keep honing pinpoint accuracy with even more movement. If your focus pads do not already have center dots on them, I suggest applying a square of duct tape for a target. During the pad drills don't just aim for the pad — strive for honing in on the dot.When you take it to the ring, pick out one or two spots on your opponent's anatomy and make those your targets of concern for your jab, Freddie Welsh-style.

8. Kid McCoy's corkscrew punch

The man born as Norman Selby in 1872, who became Charles "Kid" McCoy (another fighter's name that he causally adopted as his own), who later took on the nom de ring "The Corkscrew Kid," and then simply, "Kid McCoy," was not a good man. He was a con artist, a thief, a cheat and a hustler. His out-of-the-ring exploits could fill a book of nefarious deeds, but despite all this thuggish and disreputable baggage, you can't take away the fact that he was one of the slickest boxers to step into the ring.

Selby, McCoy or whatever name he was going by on any given day won the vacant middleweight title with a knockout in the 15th round against Dan Creedon in 1897. He never bothered to defend the title, but don't let that allow you to assume McCoy was inactive or yellow. On the contrary, he was active as hell and seemingly fearless. Consider the following:

● In 1896, the year prior to picking up the middleweight belt, he knocked out welterweight champion Tommy Ryan, a move that should have made him the champion, but he never claimed the welterweight title.

● On the evening of November 12, 1897 he knocked out George LaBlanche and Beach Ruble on the same night — both first round knockouts.

● From 1897 through 1898 he compiled 13 consecutive knockouts.

● On December 2, 1901 Kid McCoy didn't just fight three men in one night, he knocked all three out.

Let's take a look at some of the men McCoy faced. McCoy was a natural middleweight, but he took on and often did quite well against the following fighters: Joe Choynski, Tom Sharkey, Peter Maher, Jack Root, Philadelphia Jack O'Brien, Jack "Twin" Sullivan, Gus Ruhlin, and the estimable James. J. Corbett. These men were all vaunted heavyweights of the day, but McCoy had no problem saying yes to the bouts.

What McCoy lacked in good behavior he more than made up for in grit and power. McCoy could be less than ethical inside the ring, but we'll leave those stories for another day. Instead, let's focus on what gave him the nickname, "The Corkscrew Kid."

McCoy claims to have invented an altogether new punch that he dubbed the "corkscrew." He would tell many tales about where and how he developed it over the years always varying details here and there. In some incidences it was shown to him by a "Chinaman" (his words, not mine). In another version it's a lesson he picked up from watching his kitten play with a dangling toy.

The "corkscrew" is essentially a rotation of the fist as it makes contact. By adding a bit of twist at the end of a punch you can induce tearing action if timed correctly with impact. McCoy claimed (and yeah, again highly doubtful considering the source) that he could use the corkscrew tactic and punch a bag of cement and eventually grind it into a fine powder.

Numerous opponents, both horizontal and vertical, could testify to being poleaxed and/or cut by McCoy's trademark tool. We will outline the cleaner version because McCoy's version had a bit of extra help. He would wrap his hands in mounds of friction tape to give some extra heft and grab that allowed him to club and tear skin all the better. I will say that this is one of his nicer dirty tricks inside the ring. Again, stories for another day.

Throwing corkscrews
Kid McCoy-style

Commonly the corkscrew is thought of as being used only in straight punches, so that is where we'll start.

Corkscrew jab

● With a typical jab, the fist turns to the horizontal position (palm down) while travelling to the target.
● In the corkscrew jab we want to save this movement for the precise moment of impact.

● *Important:* It is not simply turning the wrist or forearm to palm-down position. We want to turn the entire arm from the shoulder as if following the rifling of a gun barrel. Learn the whole arm twist along with the timing and you'll have some major stink on this punch in no time.

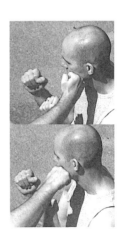

Clockwise from upper left, corkscrews off jab, rear straight, hook and uppercut.

Punch, twist and tear.

Corkscrew rear straight

● Like the timing and mechanics of the corkscrew jab.

It is commonly thought that you can corkscrew only straight punches. Au contraire! Read on and we'll get your hooks and uppercuts in on the corkscrew game.

Corkscrew lead hook

● You will want to fire the corkscrew hook with the hooking forearm parallel to the ground.
● The incoming hook travels with palm facing inward (facing you). Arc and twist to a palm-down orientation upon impact.

Corkscrew rear hook

● Follow the lead hook mechanics.

Corkscrew lead uppercut

● As your fire your lead uppercut, the fist will be in a palm-facing-you orientation.
● Upon impact, make a quick twist of the wrist from palm-facing to palm-inward.
● Be sure to drive this twist with the entire forearm and not simply from the wrist.

Corkscrew rear uppercut

● Follow the lead uppercut mechanics.

Allow a good 2-3 weeks to make the transition from traditional to corkscrew. Your arsenal may not be pulverizing bags of concrete to powder, but your punches will be that much more effective thanks to this famously infamous fighter.

9. Sandy Saddler's slashing jab

Sandy Saddler is one of THE bona fide legends of the vicious game that is boxing. He has his detractors — those who point to his occasional less-than-kosher tactics such as heeling, holding, thumbing, collaring and wrestling. But even his detractors will admit the man didn't need the outside-the-rules tactics. Saddler could BOX — the man would bring that vicious jab back to perfect position more often than most champions afflicted with the "curse" that is speed. His series of matches with another all-time great, Willie Pep, are the stuff of history.

There is a lot to learn from Mr. Saddler. His record is evidence enough of a superlative fighter. Saddler fought 162 bouts, won 144 and lost only 16 with 2 draws. But his knockout tally of 103 is perhaps the stat with the most snap. It puts him among the top 10 KO artists of all time, in all of boxing — and the most ever for featherweights.

Now, consider that KO tally and have a look at any photo of the tall, gangly Saddler. Just where did that power come from? It seems the answer may be found in some of the deliberate timing of what, from the outside, looks like an awkwardly thrown lead hand. When watching film of Saddler throw his jab, we see that often when his jab lands his opponent's head turns or bobs more than is usual upon receiving a standard jab. Normally, an unblocked jab snaps the head straight back. When Saddler's jab lands flush we see the head either torque left (Saddler threw orthodox) or bump down.

The secret to this extra bump of the opponent's head is how Saddle slashed or whipped his jab. Let's use the following drills to see if we can buy ourselves some of this unexpected power.

Throwing Sandy Saddler's slashing jab

Saddler's jab traveled a slightly inward or slightly downward arc. Yes, he often threw the traditional straight line, in-out jab, but much of Saddler's renown was for this arcing/slashing motion that could open cuts and provide a hard, torqueing wallop. Saddler's slashing angles are what provided that extra torque and stink to make his jab a bit more powerful than a traditional jab, even though it was often thrown (and intentionally so) as glancing blows.

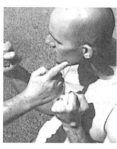

Slashing inside jab

● Throw your standard jab, but ...
● Recalibrate your landing target about one or two inches left of target for orthodox fighters (one or two inches to the right for southpaws).

● *To help you visualize:* If I want to land a jab flush on my opponent's mouth, I will target my slashing inside jab to land on the right corner of his mouth or perhaps even one inch right of that corner. I would adjust the target to the left of the mouth if I throw southpaw.

● As my jab lands, I think less of penetrating through the target and more of immediately contracting the chest and stomach muscles to drag/slash/whip the jab to the inside of the target-in-the-mouth example — as if I was going to wipe the smile off his face with my fist.

To the left is a normal, straight-line jab. The sequence below shows the angle of a slashing jab.

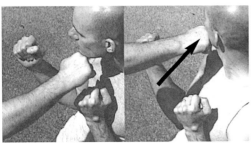

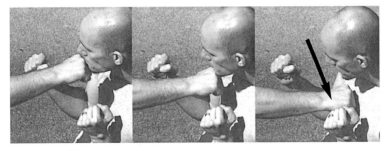

Slashing down jab

Saddler also bumped that head down with an alternate version of his slashing jab, let's look at how he did it.

● Fire your jab straight and true, but about one inch above your mark.

● Just as your jab makes contact above target, contract your abdominal and lat muscles hard to slash/rake the jab downward tearing into your target from above. Keep in mind the key to Saddler's slashing jabs is not to penetrate with the punch in the usual manner, but to slash the skin of the opponent.

I suggest honing the range and timing on the heavy bag, then take it to the pads. Initially, it may feel "off" and you may unintentionally stop your fist a few times, but once you find it, it'll pay big rewards.

Connecting the toe to the fist

Let's look to the featherweight great for another lesson. This one is so simple it almost feels like a throwaway tip, but if you work it for a week or two with diligence, you'll wonder, "Why didn't I know this from day one?"

OK, we've already covered the fact that many saw Sandy Saddler's rough and tumble style with its occasional lapse into less-than-inside-the-lines tactics as lamentable. Detractors and appreciators alike seldom point to Saddler as a graceful boxer, but no one disputes that he was a great fighter all the same.

He is often appreciated for his grit and his power, but seldom do you hear him referred to as one of the great defensive geniuses of the ring. Well, allow me to be the one to tell you that there is defensive (and offensive) genius in Saddler's stance and movement. He utilized a brilliant little trick that kept his lead hand in almost perfect position to defend or fly out with a ready offense (particularly when using either the slashing inside or slashing downward jab covered previously.)

The good news for us, is that this tip is so easy to learn it's almost laughable. What is this tip?

For an in-depth look at the history of both Sandy Saddler and Willie Pep, do yourself a favor and have a look at my friend and publisher's book *Willie Pep vs. Sandy Saddler: Notes on the Boxing Legends and Epic Rivalry.*

Saddler stood and moved as if his lead hand was connected to his lead foot. When he was standing tall with a narrow stance, that fist was tucked close to the body. When he hit a wide stance or was in active movement, we see that hand move out with his lead foot.

The key to the whole thing is when the lead hand is not being used to hit or to defend, it is still ready to do either. And to make it ready to do either Saddler-style is to envision a vertical pole protruding from the big toe of the lead foot to the lead hand. This pole is always on a strict vertical axis and never tilts in any direction.

Put that lead hand on top of that pole and voila!

Connecting the fist to the toe
Here are a few drills to get this under our belts.

Mirror work
● Get in front of the mirror and hit a few rounds of offensive and defensive movement.
● All the while strive to keep that lead fist on top of the pole when it is not in use.
● *Tip:* Go through as many wide and shallow footwork iterations as you can to seat this concept.

Bag work
● Hit the same drill on the bag.
● Work offense *and* defense. Often we fall back into old habits when we get primarily offensive with the bag.
● For several rounds bang while paying attention to the pole position.

Take it to the pads
● Same here. Whenever you or your coach catch your hand out of pole position, call it and get it where it needs to be.

This is such a simple concept, I am shocked it isn't used from day one in training. We all hear "Get those hands up!" but seldom do we hear addressed how to actively and effectively position that lead hand when on the move. Big tip of the hat to Mr. Saddler!

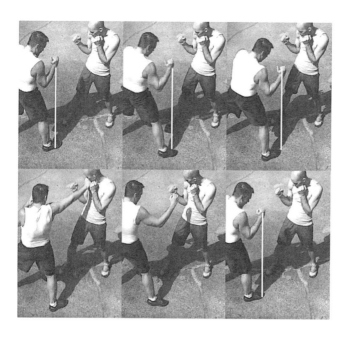

10. Tommy Loughran's fencing jabs

How good was Tommy Loughran?

This light heavyweight champion was so good that although he never scaled much more than 175 pounds, he managed to fight and defeat over the course of his career 10 champions in all divisions ranging from welterweight to heavyweight.

How good was Tommy Loughran?

He gave up 86 pounds, 6 inches in height and 12 inches in reach to face heavyweight champion Primo Carnera — the greatest weight disparity in a championship bout. Yes, Carnera was a paper champion, but he was still the bigger, stronger man. But Loughran was still there at the end of the bout and comported himself just fine at that.

How good was Tommy Loughran?

He fought two matches with the talented heavyweight Jack Sharkey. He lost the first, but took him in the rematch.

How good was Tommy Loughran?

Jack Dempsey hired him as a sparring partner to prepare for Gene Tunney because he wanted slick boxers to cut to size.

Reporters at ringside saw that it didn't go as planned for the Manassas Mauler. Sportswriters at the training camp related that Loughran nimbly avoided Dempsey's rushes and danced away with ease.

How good was Tommy Loughran?

The immortal Jack Johnson said, "The only modern boxer I know who can really pick off punches."

How good was Tommy Loughran?

In his first 117 fights he was floored only four times.

How good was Tommy Loughran?

He did all of this practically one-handed, and this is no exaggeration. At the beginning of Loughran's career he had a 50 percent knockout record (7 KOs in 14 fights.) In the 158 fights to follow he reaped only 10 knockouts.

So how did this legend climb so high with practically only one hand? Just what happened to that promising KO hand? And, what can we learn from this adaptable champ to make our own lead hand all the better?

He broke his power hand often in those early bouts, and it healed so poorly it was always in danger of further damage. Consequently Loughran threw his right seldom and used it instead to pick off punches as Jack Johnson said. We'll get to that lesson in another section, but first ...

Tommy Loughran's fencing jabs

To even approach Loughran's ability with the jab, you're going to have to throw it and throw it a lot.

5-Day, 5,000 jab challenge

It is advised to hit this challenge on nonconsecutive training days to allow your lead shoulder time to recover. Count via mental tally or use a pitch counter. It's OK to take a break now and again, but you should wind up with a total of 1,000 jabs on the given day.

Day 1: In front of a mirror flick 1,000 jabs.
Day 2: Slam a heavy bag 1,000 times with your jab.
Day 3: And 1,000 times into a double-end bag.
Day 4: Get on the move and flick the pads 1,000 times.
Day 5: Pick your device of choice (mirror, bag, double-end bag, pads) and throw 1,000 consecutive jabs nonstop! That's 1,000 jabs thrown with authority, one right after the other. Once you've hit the 5,000 your shoulder should be ready to start its Tommy Loughran education.

Stance

● Take a somewhat wider stand than normal and move weight distribution from 50/50 to around 60/40 with the lion's share of the weight going to the back foot.
● You will also take a bit of a rearward lean.
● The lead hand is positioned out over the lead toes.

Probing jab

● From this outside range and leaning away position, let's work on moving and flicking that jab.
● Don't strive to put any major stink on it, just get used to moving (a lot) and flicking the jab (a lot.)
● Again, resist the urge to lean in with the jab to increase power.
● Don't forget to throw to the head and the body.

Stop-hit jab

This is one area where Loughran excelled. Any movement from his opponent, any movement at all that resembled getting set, whether getting set to move or set to hit, earned them a jab — usually in the face.

You'll need good sparring partners who are gloved and protected for this drill.

● Have your partner move and look to hit. Controlled, of course, since this is a learning stroke drill.
● Anytime you see something that even hints at being a movement, throw a jab.
● Even if you turn out to be wrong in your prediction, throw a jab.

The goal is not so much to counterpunch as it is to be there before anything gets off. Or to be there while their punch is on the way. Your jab landing before theirs acts as a post or push-off, removing much of the stink of their incoming shot.

Don't be afraid to throw. You've got to learn to have confidence to throw often. But more importantly, to throw Loughran's fencing jab, you've got to throw as they get set or as their punch is coming in. It's a subtle distinction, but one well worth making and educating.

Tommy Loughran's jab and a half

Ready for another lesson from the great Tommy Loughran? This one is rather easy to get under your belt and just might drive your coach a little bit crazy because it strays from strict good form. But once we put Loughran's fencing jabs together with the jab and a half, then we add the catcher's mitt tactic — Oh, we'll be cooking with gas!

● Get in front of the bag or mirror and each time you throw the jab, allow that rear hand to travel half the distance of the jab's trajectory.
● Keep that rear hand open in catcher's mitt fashion.
● Work this drill for several rounds to get used to the odd mechanics of throwing both hands out at the same time.
● *Tip:* I find that driving off the toes of the rear foot from Loughran's rearward leaning stance makes it feel less that you are simply reaching with both hands.

Tommy Loughran's catcher's mitt

Now that we have Tommy Loughran's omnipresent jab under our belts as well as the jab and a half tactic, let's make your rear hand do some more work as Tommy's lead hand did not work alone. Sound like a contradiction? After all, didn't we just learn that he broke his rear hand and that he seldom threw it?

Yes, that's all true, but it does not mean that Loughran didn't use that hand. He used it almost as often as the lead hand — he just seldom punched with it. Let's recall the great Jack Johnson's opinion of Tommy Loughran: "The only modern boxer I know who can really pick off punches."

When we see Tommy jab we also see that rear hand come out with it, not quite as far as the jab, but it makes its presence known — this is our jab and a half.

Loughran used this rear hand as a quasi catcher's mitt or proactive muffler to allow him to jab as often as he did and slow the other fighter's roll, so to speak.

Let's look to some drills to build this interesting skill.

Tommy Loughran's catcher's mitt drills

Each of these are ideally worked with a training partner because they rely on the live feedback that bag and mirror work cannot provide.

Catcher's mitt

● Throw a pulled jab, that is, one without a lot of stink on it as the nature of the drill means your partner is allowing his or her head to be bait — have some courtesy.

● As you throw the jab, keep your chin tucked behind that lead shoulder to protect against a rear hand and ...

● Allow the rear hand to come forward approximately half the distance of the jab in preparation to catch a counter jab.

● Your partner should strive to get off a jab as you are firing so you can get used to this simultaneous movement.

● *Note:* Loughran' s catcher's mitt didn't drift out only when he anticipated a jab, he moved it out almost each and every time. So in essence, you are practically always throwing the jab and a half we covered earlier.

Jab and muffle

If you do not encounter a counter jab on the way in with your jab and a half, you still put that rear hand to work.

● If you meet no incoming punch, place the open glove or heel of the glove on your partner's shoulder or biceps to muffle his counter.

● *Tip:* I suggest working the catcher's mitt drill and the jab and muffle in isolation before combining them. Let's really seat both sides of this jab and a half equation before we assume we have it tight.

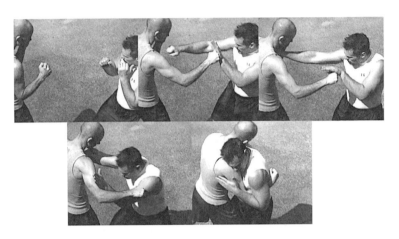

Catch to clinch

● With your partner and while firing the jab and a half, use your catch hand to swim to a clinch.

● Allow the catch hand to follow the caught hand back and over-hook the arm to the clinch.

● The jab arm will only retract partially and use it's own muffle to ride in and secure the clinch on the other side.

Muffle to clinch

● Splitting hairs here, but practice makes perfect.

● Throw the jab and a half and when your catcher's mitt finds no incoming to catch, use it to muffle the shoulder or biceps and follow to a clinch.

● Secure the clinch on the opposite side with the jab hand as in the preceding drill.

● *Tip:* Once you are able to catch to clinch and muffle to clinch Loughran-style, it's time to combine all of these into several rounds of sparring where you seek to land your jab OFTEN and catch and muffle and clinch to your partner's endless frustration. Never think you are muffling, catching or clinching too often. To play the game Tommy Loughran-style, do it again and again and again — and then do it some more.

> In that historic 12th round, Conn caught the bigger, stronger man with an exchange that stunned Louis ...

11. Billy Conn's hit and run

Born William David Conn, Jr. in East Liberty, Pennsylvania, Billy Conn, aka "The Pittsburgh Kid" was a very talented light heavyweight champion, but his name will be forever linked to his two attempts to outbox and cut the then heavyweight champion down to size. And this wasn't just any ol' heavyweight champion. This was "The Brown Bomber," the immortal Joe Louis.

Conn was never a hard hitter. As a matter of fact, his record shows only 14 knockouts out of a total of 76 bouts. So what was it that made Billy Conn think that he as a relatively light hitting, light heavy could step up and take it to one of the all-time greats?

There are three answers to that question:
1. He had guts.
2. He had speed.
3. He had a beautifully deceptive defensive style that kept him out of trouble more often than not.

Conn met Louis for the first time on June 18, 1941. The official weigh-in has them listed as Conn 174 pounds and Louis 199 1/2 pounds. Some sources in the know report the actual weights on fight night were 169 to 204. Either way you cut it, Conn was giving up at least 25 1/2 pounds, maybe 35 pounds, and he was giving up this weight to a world champion — a hard-hitting one with 52 knockouts to his credit.

To be fair, most of the fight saw Conn on the move, but this was his "hit and run" style as he called it. To which the champion famously responded "He can run, but he can't hide." Turns out Conn did a pretty good job of hiding for the first 12 rounds. In that historic 12th round, Conn caught the bigger, stronger man with an exchange that stunned Louis and sent him back to his championship stool flat footed.

In the 13th, Conn abandoned what had worked to that point, his trademark hit and run, and decided to trade a little. Bad call. The bigger, stronger and rightfully renowned heavyweight champion found him with hard shots and dropped Conn with only two seconds left in the unlucky-for-Conn, but lucky-for-Louis 13th round.

He may have lost his bid for the heavyweight title, but this is one of those cases where even a loss is a victory. Let's have a look at Conn's hit and run and see if we can develop some of it ourselves to better our game when facing bigger, stronger opponents.

Building the hit and run

First, let's take a root combination and work it as a power pyramid. We'll use a jab/cross/lead hook/rear uppercut combo that can also be written as J/C/H/RU. Hit the following drills in front of the mirror.

In-and-out power pyramid
● Lunge-step in, fire a jab and lunge-step retreat immediately.
● Lunge-step in and fire the J/C, lunge-step retreat.
● Lunge-step J/C/H, lunge-step retreat.
● Lunge-step J/C/H/RU, lunge-step retreat.
● Repeat the pyramid and movement pattern until the designated rounds are complete.

Lunge, jab, retreat

Lunge, jab, cross, retreat

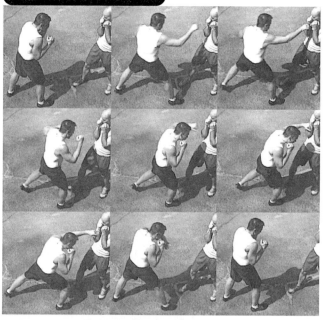

Lunge, jab, cross, hook, retreat

Lunge, jab, cross, hook, uppercut, retreat

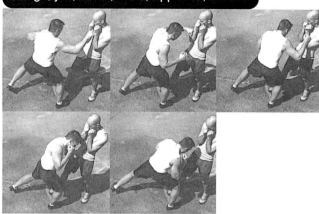

Wheel-out power pyramid

● Lunge-step in and fire the jab.
● Wheel the rear foot to the outside (your back) and retreat.
● Repeat this sequence pyramiding through the root combination (jab/cross, jab/cross/hook, jab/cross/hook/uppercut).

Jab, wheel-out

Jab, cross, wheel-out

Jab, cross, hook, wheel-out

Jab, cross, hook, uppercut, wheel-out

Wheel-in power pyramid

● Lunge-step in and fire the jab.
● This time wheel to the inside (toward your chest) before retreating
● Like before, continue the pattern with all the combinations.

Jab, wheel-in

In-and-out plus wheeling free form

● Adhere to the power pyramid, but switch it up on each exit: lunge-step retreat, wheel-in or wheel-out.
● *Next:* Take this same drill progression to the heavy bag and then have your coach/partner give you an active feed with the pads. Once you have run this root combination, feel free to insert any combination you desire and put it through the same paces. If you adhere to these steps you'll be hitting and running Billy Conn-style in no time.

Billy Conn's defensive rock and roll

There was more to Billy Conn's style then simply hitting and running. After all, no matter how speedy you are there are times when you are inside that you will get caught. And Conn was caught by the bigger, stronger Louis in his historic meetings with the champ. And I'm not talking about the punches that finally floored him, but all of the others in rounds 1-12 that Conn survived.

> He was a master of the rock and roll, the small motions of the upper body and legs that act as shock absorbers ...

Conn, like Tommy Loughran, was another defensive wizard. But Conn's wizardry took on a different form than Loughran's fencing and catcher's mitt style. Conn would use a relaxed shell position to receive incoming punches on his arms, elbows and gloves.

If it were only easy as shelling we wouldn't even mention it, but any of us who have been hit knows that even getting banged in a shell hurts and steals power and snap from our own punches. Conn didn't just shell. He was a master of the rock and roll, the small motions of the upper body and legs that act as shock absorbers to eat up the power of incoming punches.

First let's examine Conn's shell position, the one he used as he entered and exited with his hit and run style.

Billy Conn's loose shell
● Bring the rear hand to the cheek.
● Tuck that chin into the lead shoulder.
● Bring the lead hand approximately 8 inches in front of the lead shoulder.
● Keep the forearms parallel.

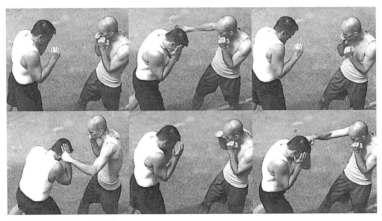

Pat down drill
● Gear up and have your coach/partner use the pads or 16 ounce gloves to lightly throw all manner of punches at you.
● Your goal is to defend via footwork and the smallest movement of the arms within this shell.

Conn rock

● Versus straight punches Conn would allow the punch to be absorbed on his shell as he pinched his gloves and forearms together.

● At the same time he would change weight distribution from 50/50 upon either leg to 60/40, putting more weight on his rear leg.

● This can be accomplished simply by dropping the rear heel a bit (that heel should normally be up).

● As soon as you have absorbed the straight punch with the rock, rock back to the 50/50 position.

Pat down drill part 2

● Assume a loose shell and have your partner throw a few rounds of light straight shots to head and body as you work the timing of Conn's rock.

Conn roll to the lead side of head or body

● To receive hooks to head or body you'll need to move a bit away from them, but Conn often used a subtle movement of the upper body that was actually triggered from the feet to eat away the hook angle's energy.

● To roll away from hooks to the lead side of the body, drop your rear foot flat to the floor. Doing so leaves you in perfect 50/50 weight distribution without any need of adding excessive lean to the upper body.

Conn roll to the rear side of head or body

● To receive shots from this side, use the toes of the rear foot to drive your weight forward and to the outside as you allow your lead knee to descend no more than 3-4 inches.

● Immediately use your lead leg to snap back to a 50/50 weight distribution.

Pat down drill part 3

● Have your partner work you over with both hook angles to head and body as you seat both side rolls.

Pat down drill part 4

● Have your partner lightly fire straight and hook angles to the head and body as you work on combining the rock and roll. And last, but certainly not least ...

Hit and run rock and roll sparring

● Agree to light contact as you strive to work your power pyramid hit and run tactics.

● Your partner has permission to fire back lightly.

● Strive to use the loose shell and rock and roll to control the impact.

● If you keep it honest and run the drills with close attention to detail, we can steal a little of that crafty Conn magic.

Billy Conn's hare trigger

Another lesson from the crafty Billy Conn? Yes indeedy. And is that a typo or a pun in the name of this lesson? A pun, but one with a bit of meaning to it.

Billy Conn's hit and run style combined with his rock and roll defense also gives rise to an ability to get off quickly following a defense. It is not so much a counterpunch style as a "triggering" counter tripped by your opponent's incoming shot. There were and there are still many fine speedy legends who use this trigger boxing method and Conn utilized it as well as anybody.

Building a hare trigger

To throw trigger counters we've got to come to grips with the idea that rather than muffling and being proactive Tommy Loughran-style, you are using the Conn loose shell and responding ASAP upon rocking and rolling with an incoming punch.

In each of the following drills as soon as you receive and absorb the prescribed punch, fire back immediately with the prescribed punch or combination.

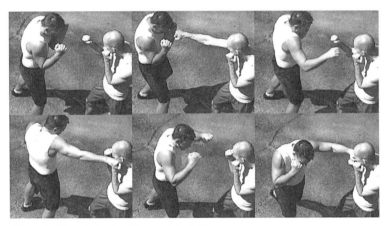

Rock the jab to the old 1-2

● Gear up, both you and your partner.
● Your partner will trigger with jabs to the head or body.
● As soon as you rock with the jab spring back with a jab/cross combination.

Rock the rear straight to the 2-3

● Your partner will fire the straight rear hand.
● You will shell and rock and then ...
● Return fire with your own rear straight and lead hook.

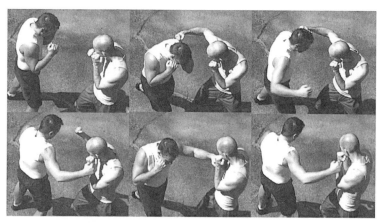

Roll the lead hook to the 3-2-3

● Your partner will fire lead hooks to the head or body.
● Shell and roll and as your toes bring you back to position ...
● Fire a lead hook, rear straight, lead hook combination.

Roll the rear hook to the 2-3-2

● Your partner will fire a rear hook to head or body.
● Shell, roll and come back with ...
● A rear straight, lead hook, and then another rear straight.

Roll the rear hook to lead uppercut

Conn was also mighty comfortable returning a rear hook for a rear hook. We will do the same and add a lead uppercut. When our hook lands, we will have pulled his chin to our lead hand.

● Your partner will fire a rear hook to the head or body.
● Shell and roll and return fire …
● Rear hook to lead uppercut.

Hare trigger free form drill

● In this drill your feeder will cut his speed to 50 percent to begin with as you rock and roll and apply the prescribed trigger sequences.
● Your partner is firing his shots at random.

Once comfortable at 50 percent, climb to 75, 85 and finally 100 percent. Walk these drill steps and you will find yourself becoming proficient at hare triggering like the great and gutsy Billy Conn.

12. Pancho Villa's hook-jab

One word comes to mind when one thinks of the gentleman born Francisco Gulliedo. That word is speed.

This future flyweight champion was born in the Philippines in 1901 with fighting in his blood. As a very young man he chose to leave his small town of Lloilo on the island of Panay for the big city of Manila where he could compete more often in novatos, which translates loosely to novices, or fights for beginners. Basically these novatos served as young Francisco's Golden Gloves education.

He was so devoted to the idea of becoming a fighter and competing in the novatos that he slept on the streets and shined shoes during the day. He trained when he could and took on any novato that came his way.

This determination paid off as it allowed him to move to the United States where he climbed up the flyweight ladder. He earned a shot at the champion Jimmy Wilde (no slouch himself) who he knocked out in the 7th round in 1923.

Along the way Franciso picked up the ring name Pancho Villa and a reputation for being a hard-living, fun-loving guy who was there to make the most of it in the ring and in the nightclubs as well. It was the Roaring Twenties and Pancho was a young man ready to roar.

He became the toast of New York. At the clubs he would occasionally hold court playing either the drums or the ukulele. Sometimes he seemed to be burning the candle at both ends, but when he hit the ring, that candle still burned hot and it burned FAST. We mentioned his speed, right?

Pancho's career was cut short when he succumbed to an infection caused by infected teeth. A wisdom tooth extraction exacerbated the problem. The champ was felled at the age of 24 by something that could now be knocked out with a dose of antibiotics. He lived fast, he died young and we have much to learn from him.

Pancho Villa must have picked up many tricks in his uncountable novatos because he did very interesting things with a lead hand that he carried precariously low.

Let's review how he threw his jab-hook hybrid.

Pancho Villa's hook-jab

Pancho broke one of the tenets that we tout in this book: KEEP YOUR HANDS UP! Pancho usually fought from a lead hand low guard. But fortunately for us, it is not necessary to throw his hook-jab from this precarious position. Most of us lack his speed, so we will wisely choose to throw it from high guard.

The hook-jab (above) does not extend straight from the shoulder like a normal jab (right).

Hook-jab mechanics

Pancho used this loose hook almost exclusively in place of a standard jab. It's a punch that sort of splits the difference between a straight jab and a long hook. Let's look at how it's done.

● When you raise the elbow as if to fire a standard jab ...

● Allow the lead hand to drift about three inches to the outside of your lead shoulder.

● Fire the hooking jab from this outside orientation.

● Don't keep the elbow locked and rigid as you would in a standard hook.

● Although it travels in a hooking trajectory, it will still have more of a jab finish on it.

● *Note:* It penetrates and does not slash as in Sandy Saddler's jab. A little bit of work with this one on both the heavy bag and pads will seat this skill fairly easily.

Pancho Villa's double left or double lead

The speedy champion could double up on his lead hook with little or no telegraphing. Let's allow Pancho to describe the double left in his own words:

"My best punch is my double left. First I hook the body, and then, with the same movement, I hook the jaw. It was how I surprised 'The [Johnny] Buff.' When I hooked him to the stomach he expected me to step back. But I no step back. Instead, I hook him to the chin with the same hand, and 'The Buff,' him drop to the mat."

Clever stuff here. Hooks usually require counter revolution or a shuffle step to fire the second hooking angle. But Pancho doubles his up, and it still has power. Exactly where is that power coming from?

Most of us can't fire one hook and simply send the second to the chin and drop a champion, which Johnny Buff was at the time (American flyweight champion). There's a subtle magic going on here that Pancho left out of his description.

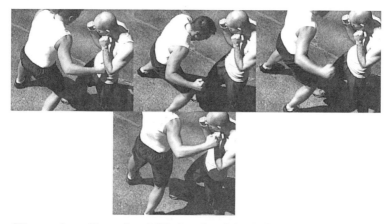

Throwing Pancho Villa's double left

Since we are not stepping to power the second hook, it turns out the secret is in four inches of elbow movement and the angle of that movement.

● Throw a standard lead hook to the body and then …
● Once it has landed, retract the elbow approximately 3-4 inches …
● Not outward, away from your opponent, but rather downward.
● Accomplish this by splitting the difference — two inches of retraction from the arm, the other two inches taken up by a slight dip in the lead knee.
● These two small motions in tandem provide a four-inch retraction.
● From the retraction point, fire the next hook straight to the jaw accompanied by an upward snap of the lead knee and hip.
● The second hook will travel in an angled upward motion.

This little subtly is what gives that double left such a wallop. You can learn this one on the bag easily before taking it to the pads.

13. Sonny Liston's hammer hook

Sonny Liston will be remembered to many from the photo of him lying prostrate on the canvas with a victorious then-Cassius Clay standing over him. I'll admit it is an iconic image, one hard to forget.

That photo, being dropped by a so-called "phantom" punch, rumors of a fix, and so on have tarnished the image of a man once considered one of the most fearsome heavyweights in history. We mustn't forget that pre-Cassius Clay, Sonny was believed to be almost unbeatable.

Liston had a troubled life. He spent time in prison for a spate of robberies as "The Yellow Shirt Bandit." He served his time and turned to boxing, but he never really left his shady doings and associates behind. He died of a heroin overdose.

Let's leave the tragic soap opera behind and look at the athlete himself. He was certainly one bad dude. Almost every photo of the man captures a brooding presence, one dripping with bad intentions. The young Mike Tyson had two heros, Jack Dempsey and Sonny Liston. He could not have chosen more suitable personas to emulate and bare to his terrified opponents.

Liston was comfortable with his image as less-than-cuddly and said so:

"A prizefight is like a cowboy movie. There has to be a good guy and a bad guy. Peoples pay their money to see me lose. Only, in my cowboy movie, the bad guy always wins."

Yet when Liston first started boxing, he was not so scary.

Oh, he had his wins, but his knockout record was less than stellar. And then something happened.

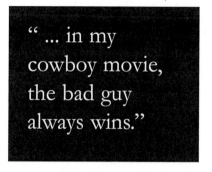

" ... in my cowboy movie, the bad guy always wins."

He broke his jaw and lost a fight to Marty Marshall in 1954. This seems to have awakened the slumbering beast. After that loss he went on a 26-fight winning streak including two wins over the jaw-breaking Marshall.

Twenty-one of those wins were by knockout. This earned him a shot at the heavyweight title, then held by Floyd Patterson. He destroyed Patterson and become the first man to win the title via a first-round knockout. He repeated with a round one KO in the rematch to retain his title.

His next fight was his downfall at the hands of the future Muhammad Ali, but let's skip that for today and turn to what made Liston so fearsome up to that point. We could start with his jolting jab and dissect those bombs he called uppercuts, but let's begin with his hammering hook.

Liston was a hard puncher. How hard? H-A-R-D! That tight lead hook came in with every bit of his formidable frame behind it along with some beautiful mechanics.

Let's look at how he did it.

Hammer hook mechanics

● Raise your lead elbow parallel to the floor.

● The fist essentially stays where it is, as if rotating in front of you on a ball-and-socket joint.

● The elbow has a strict 90-degree bend that locks the arm into one fused piece of bone.

● Hinging and pivoting on the ball of the rear-foot …

● Fire a pivot from the toes of the lead foot and turn the entire body as one unit to the inside. Shoulders, chest and hips all move as one.

● The entire body is a fused unit that drives the fused-elbow hammer hook home.

Slam the door drill

The following drill leaves the punch itself out and helps seat the skill.

- Think of your upper body as a door.
- Your rear foot is the door hinge.
- Slam this door (your chest) by …
- Driving off the toes of the lead foot.
- Drive HARD, slamming the door/chest with maximum viciousness.

Once you have mastered slamming the door, add the fused-bone mechanics of the hammer hook and be prepared for some Sonny Liston power upgrade.

14. The Mike Gibbons reconnaissance book

In this section we get deep inside the mind of a great fighter and learn to put one of the best boxing brains to work for us.

This might be a bit of a cheat because Mike Gibbons never held a title, although he claimed a portion of the middleweight title in the mad dash following the murder of the formidable Stanley Ketchel. His middleweight claim was never universally recognized, but this man known as "The St. Paul Phantom," and "The Wizard" fought more than a dozen champs and did quite well. Gibbons, as his twin fight names suggest, was more of a defensive "be there and then be gone" fighter than a "swarm in and unleash the hounds of hell" type. He owned a wickedly clever evasive style and do not let the lack of a title fool you. He fought most of the best men of his time in the no decision (ND) era — as long as both fighters were standing at the end, no winner was declared. The best that could be mustered by the end of many of his bouts was the unsatisfying ND, which are two letters nowhere near as definitive or glorious as KO.

Our non-champion faced such greats as Packey McFarland, Jack Dillon, Ted "Kid" Lewis and the great Harry Greb. We'll allow a comment from Harry Greb to his manager in the midst of one of his bouts with Gibbons to get an insight into how Mike Gibbons fought. After yet another frustrating round of chasing Gibbons around the ring and being peppered with long-range blows, Greb screamed to his corner, "You son of a bitch, from now on match me with one guy at a time!"

Mike Gibbon's artistry was translatable as he also coached his younger brother Tommy Gibbons. As a matter of fact, he coached him so well that Tommy fought the formidable Jack Dempsey to a standstill in 1922. No mean feat that.

What we want to learn from Mr. Gibbons (and his brother, Tommy) is not so much the physical ring artistry of which there is plenty to emulate, but the essence of their analytical minds — the intelligence they brought to bear in assessing, studying and breaking down opponents before they even entered the ring.

> The Gibbons boys were far more than fight analysts — they behaved more as behavioral analysts with a side interest in boxing.

The Gibbons brothers kept notes and created a book of opposition research on every fighter they had met or might meet in the future. As Mike Gibbons said, "Every bit of strength that a fighter is known to have is jotted down. Along with his weaknesses, temperamental aspects, habits, and how they are liable to affect their ring work."

This analysis goes beyond the mere watching of fight films. The Gibbons boys wanted to know if their opponents' carousing would affect how well they boxed on a weekend night as opposed to a weekday bout. They noted if they were easily upset by choice of dressing rooms or if they were bothered by winter or summer weather. The Gibbons boys were far more than fight analysts — they behaved more as behavioral analysts with a side interest in boxing.

To capture a bit of this observational wisdom, I offer the following questionnaire that you can use to begin scouting your own opponents' strengths and weaknesses. The given questions are not the only ones that can be asked. Use your own powers of observation to add to and expand the list. I mean for it to be used as a template to get inside how Mike and Tommy approached the game.

Mike Gibbons opposition survey

Opponent's name:

Ring name (If any):

Record:

Wins:

Losses:

Draws:

Knockouts:

Height:

Weight:

Reach:

Orthodox or southpaw stance:

Ambidextrous?

If he switches stance, what does it mean? (Often a stance shift foretells a given tactic. What has it meant in past fights?)

Does your opponent use his height to advantage or does he seem to find it something to be overcome?

Does he have a history of struggling with weight cuts?

Best punch:

Weakest punch:

Most thrown punch:

Least thrown punch:

How often does he clinch?

Does he use his weight in the clinch?

Boxing Like the Champs

Is he a boxer or a slugger?

Does he rush or snipe from long range?

What is his demeanor in the corner pre-fight: Calm, nervous, aggressive?

What is his demeanor in the corner between rounds?

Does he have a corner man they favor? How much does he listen?

Do they come out strong and fade?

Come out cautious and build?

Strong and stay strong?

Cagey throughout?

Does he have a tell when they throw the jab? (Example: The shoulder dips pre-throw, or it swims a little to the inside on retraction, that sort of thing.)

Does he have a tell before any given punch or tactic?

Is his footwork more step and slide?

Shuffling?

Light and bouncy?

Do changes in his footwork provide a tell for a given tactic?

How has he behaved after a win?

After a loss?

After a draw?

Does he prefer to enter the ring first or second?

Do his trunks or robe feature a favorite "lucky" color? (Sometimes simply adopting the opponent's lucky color can provide a bit of confusion. Seize every advantage.)

Write down everything you know about his training camp. Good habits, bad habits, etc.

Does he move before they punch? After?

Does he have a predominant direction of movement?

What position will you most likely find his hands in the first round?

If he breaks hand position has it been an indicator of something in past fights?

Does he work the body more than head hunting?

Has he seemed more affected by body shots or blows to the head in past fights?

How often has he looked at the clock in past fights?

Has it meant anything? (Tiredness or timing a closing flurry, for example.)

How often does he look at the referee?

Has it meant anything?

How often does he look to their corner?

Has it meant anything?

Does he talk while mixing it up?

If so, can it be timed?

Does he make an unusual sound while punching or receiving blows?

If so, is it something worth thinking about mimicking?

By all means, add your own questions as you see fit. As you can see by using the Gibbons' idea of extreme observation, there may be more to dissecting an opponent than simply using our jab.

Inside the mind of Mike Gibbons, Part 2

Let's go a little deeper inside the brilliant mind of our "non-champ," Mike Gibbons. And again, let's not let the lack of a title dissuade. The esteemed boxing historian Nat Fleischer said that Mike Gibbons was the "nearest approach to the superb artistry of Tommy Ryan that the middleweight division ever boasted." High praise, indeed.

We already know that Mike and his brother Tommy kept a book of opposition research to break down their opponents both inside and outside the ring, but if they had stopped there all this accrued information might be mere trivia. It is what they did with their intel that shows just how brilliant they were. We don't actually have the Gibbons book to hold in our hands and treasure the wisdom, but we do have a few of his comments to build a foundation.

"The tough fellow, the slugger who is willing to tear at you, must be made to back up. The clever fellow who is anxious to stand at long-range and exchange his 'Long-Toms' with you, must be made to come to you."

Using the above jewel from Mr. Gibbons, let's assume we have started our own opposition surveys on likely opponents and take the next step in making our own strategy book — a book of ring generalship.

Ring generalship, Mike Gibbons-style

Mr. Gibbons started us down the road to smart fighting with the preceding quote, so let's allow him to start our book of strategy.

"The tough fellow, the slugger who is willing to tear at you, must be made to back up."

Bang on observation! Sluggers find much of their power in their boldness, in their brash "I'm coming for ya" approach. If we can find a way to halt this advance or move it onto its heels, then we have gone a long way to mitigating the slugger's power, and done much to upset his game.

> We must endeavor to not let our opponent fight his or her fight.

"The clever fellow who is anxious to stand at long-range and exchange his 'Long-Toms' with you, must be made to come to you."

Again, absolutely brilliant! "Long-Toms" (long arms) are useful because they enable a fighter to stay on the outside and do what they do where they can't be touched. If we can make the outside fighter move to the inside, the punches must be more angular and less linear and in essence change an outside game to an inside game.

In order to get him to come to you, your game may become one of drawing, that is, providing false openings to bait him to come in. You might also try shelling up and braving out a lull to see if you can get your man to come to you. These two observations lead us to one maxim after the other.

It is not enough to fight your fight. We must endeavor to not let our opponent fight his or her fight. If we fight only our fight, then there is no need for opposition research or ring generalship or, and I'll say it, intelligence. Simply fighting your fight is to be an automaton. What we want to do is, yes, fight our fight, but let's make one aspect of fighting our fight not fighting our opponent's fight.

Rush the reluctant "Long-Tom."

If you can't get that tall fighter to come to you, you'll have to get inside. Rush inside and stay inside. Long range is where he is comfortable. Take that from him.

Stick and move!

Three of the most important words in boxing language. When feeling out our opponent, stick them with that jab and then move. That move can be a side step, a slide step, a dance away, a slip, a bob-and-weave, hell it could be a back flip for all you care. Your job is to stick and move. One punch thrown usually gets a punch in return, don't be where you were when you last punched. If this sounds like I've just rephrased stick and move, pat yourself on the back for being an intelligent fighter.

A rusher earns a one-two

When facing a down-the-pipe rusher, stick that jab while side stepping, and toss that rear straight in for good measure. Hey, was that stick and move again? Yes, it was.

Knockouts need room

Knockout punches require the fist to do a bit of travelling to build enough force to do the job. This doesn't mean that all swings need to come from somewhere in Iowa, but it does mean at least 8-10 inches are required for a schooled boxer to get off what he needs to do. That distance doesn't sound like much, does it? But consider that we've all banged the bag or pads and have had the experience where the feeder or bag swing brought our fist into contact a little sooner than we expected. Not that satisfying was it?

We time our punches, we see our target and zero in for the impact to be at a given distance. When that distance is cut we are not at full power or maximum force. If we can steal a bit of that puncher's room we can steal a bit of his power. With that in mind …

... don't be where you were when you last punched.

When a rusher gets close, you get even closer

When we get caught flat footed and can't get our stick and move game going, do the unexpected and steal his room.

Hands up!

If you've got a good coach you should be hearing "Hands up!" more often than at a muggers convention. Why, oh, why does this ever have to be said? That glove in your face should be the feedback that says, "Apparently my hands were a bit low." If your opponent has a good jab that is used often, get those hands up! Keep the rear glove high and in position, ready to catch whatever is thrown.

Don't be a head hunter

The pursuit of the almighty knockout leads some to concentrate their attacks on the head because we all know that the jaw is the key to the KO more often than not. Kill the body and the head will follow.

Riposte!

A riposte is a quick clever reply in the world of insults. In the world of fencing it is a return thrust following a parry. In boxing it is a quick counterpunch or counter combination following a jab. Usually you will slip or duck that jab and then hit your riposte to the head or body. Your job as an intelligent boxer is to riposte like a master. Oh, and while slipping and ducking — hands up!

Steal the jabber's room
Yeah, broken record I know, but that jab has a range on it. Steal that range. Back your opponent to the corner or to the ropes and take away their optimum jab range.

The center of the ring is high ground, own it!
The fighter not in the center of the ring will have his or her back closer to the ropes or a corner. That means there is a possibility of being driven to the ropes or corner. When you have been driven from the center of the ring, the first thing to do is to regain this high ground position. When you have the center of the ring, start planning your drive to get him on the ropes or into a corner.

Do not slug with a slugger!
All the best sluggers in history have loved a trade war. This is the fight they want, Don't give it to them. Instead ...

Keep moving!
Sluggers need to set and throw. You can steal a lot of the slugger's efficacy by constant movement that steals his set up.

In and out!
Move, but don't run away. You've got to fight, but the way to do it is with quick in and out attacks. Don't stick around, that's the slugger's game. Steal his game.

Circle away from the power

The rear hand is the most dangerous hand, circling into it is a recipe for disaster. Circle away from the power.

Make the unmatched lead come to you

When fighting a southpaw, or you as a southpaw fighting an orthodox stance, jab and make them come to you. Probe to watch how they move. Don't assume the game will be the same.

> ... if you don't have the gas in the tank, you are halfway to losing ...

A lead hook is your best friend versus an unorthodox stance

When fighting a matched lead fighter, your rear straight is often THE bomb to throw. When you are in unmatched leads, that lead hook becomes the new bomb. Time their jab, slip outside and blast that hook!

Conditioning is your best punch

I don't care how strong you are, I don't care how fast you are, I don't care how much experience you have — if you don't have the gas in the tank, you are halfway to losing before you step into the ring.

Relax

Easier said than done because there will be pain when you step into the ring. But remember, your opponent will be nervous, too. Your job is not to have zero emotions, that's impossible. Your job is simply to be cooler and calmer than the person in front of you.

Tried and true is true for a reason

Stick to the basics, hew to the fundamentals. Keep your hands up. Stick and move. Keep the high ground. The coolest, baddest, most show-boaty thing out there ain't nothing without the fundamentals.

Fighters get hit, good fighters don't get hit as much

If you expect to make it through a fight unscathed, you are living on a planet that never existed. Boxing is a contact sport. It's a combat sport. Some bumps and bruises are inevitable. Don't stress about how to never get hurt. Focus on doling out punishment and being on the receiving end as little as possible. And what you do receive, weather it well. How do you weather it well, you may ask?

Get your Game face on

You're in a fight, and you're gonna get hurt. The game is about hitting and there is no way around the fact that you will get hit at some point, and in some bouts hit often. Getting hit hurts, but it is in your best interest to suck it up and don't show it.

Showing you're hurt is encouragement to your opponent just when you don't want him to be encouraged. You want time to recover. Showing you're hurt tells the person in front of you "Maybe I should move in and do more of what just worked."

Keeping your game face just may give you the time and opportunity to get yourself back together and back into the fight. Keep in mind, you're both getting hit; you're both getting hurt.

When you are hurt, don't say you're not hurt, just keep your game face on

If after a solid blow your opponent says or waves it off as if "That ain't nothing," chances are it was something. Announcing you are fine is simply another way of saying, "Yeah that was a good one, better than the others have been, but I'm still in here." I get wanting to express that sentiment, but all the better to shut your mouth and keep fighting your game. Make your opponent wonder, "What's it gonna take to get this guy outta here?"

> Being in range is your trigger to throw those hands.

Follow the leader

Your lead hand is the closest weapon you've got to your opponent. It gets there faster than the rear hand and therefore is harder to defend. Use that lead hand. It's called a lead because it's the leader. Let your offense and defense stack up behind this leader and make this leader lead from the front in an aggressively active way.

Fights are won in the gym, not in the ring

This maxim is a call back to both having your conditioning in order and the fact that your strategy and tactics had better have been worked out in the gym with hours and hours of repetitive training. If you wait until you are in the ring to "figure your man out" you are a least 30 days behind schedule.

Two words: keep moving

Do not stay still. Stick and move. Even if you're too tired to stick a jab in someone's face, move anyway. Staying still will get you hit. Not getting hit should be motivation enough to move.

HANDS UP!

Didn't we already cover this? Yeah, but have a look at most fights from amateur to pro. Once we get tired, once we get cocky we need to be told again: HANDS UP!!!

Half a punch is 100 percent wasted effort

If you are going to throw a punch, you are expending energy. So why would we expend energy with something that has no damaging intent on it? Every half effort eats into reserves that could be used for full effect. And no, I'm not saying save it up. I'm saying even when fatigue says, "I'll throw something lackluster here," suck it up, dig deep and throw something bona fide. That dig-deep punch just may be what the doctor ordered.

When in range — PUNCH!

Why? Because the person not punching is a person getting punched. Being in range is your trigger to throw those hands.

The best defense is a good offense ... usually

When you step into the ring you are there to meet someone who has the exact same goal as you — to punch another human being into submission. In essence, there are really only two modes in boxing (and I'm being simplistic here), offense and defense.

Counterpunching is a tough skill to master (and one we should all strive to master) so the odds say that most fighters will need to defend and then respond. If you make it your goal to "keep them on the defensive," then you've gone a long way to racking up the points and removing much of the opportunity of being hit.

Punches in bunches

Combinations are where it's at. The jab is manna, but something behind the jab is even better, even if it's only another jab. Punch often.

> Master the positive and negative aspects of all your punches.

You will miss more than you hit

Opponents aren't heavy bags or focus mitts. Opponents are real-live athletes who have some major motivation to make you miss. Watch any fight from amateur to pro and you will see more punches miss than hit. We must make sure our training addresses good recovery. Throw those hands well with malicious intent, but make sure they are retracted fast and sure. Master the positive and negative aspects of all your punches.

Change it up

This is like the "I before E except after C" rule in spelling. Yes, stick to the basics, know and use the fundamentals, but it is wise to throw some spice into the stew to keep the opponent guessing. If you throw the same things in the same way over and over again, you will be timed and you will be hit. Nobody likes to be hit.

Upset the set fighter

All fighters (you included) need to set up to throw, that's just physics, body mechanics and leverage.

All of us have our little tells before we throw. When a fighter gets set, be gone. Move. Get out of the way. Upset his set pattern. Even better if you stick 'em with a jab while you leave.

We could keep going on for days, but these bits of wisdom compiled Mike Gibbons-style, if followed scrupulously, will make us smarter fighters.

Historical training and conditioning

Now let's turn the spotlight on a few training methods used by past masters. Some of these are unusual, others are interesting twists on old standards.

15. Stanley Ketchel, rotational power and boulders

Stanley Ketchel, aka, "The Michigan Assassin," was truly one of the greatest middleweight champions of all time. He was noted for tremendous power in both hands that he threw often. Almost any description of Ketchel's punching power penned by sportswriters of the time echoes this one from Bert Randolph Sugar:

"Like Dempsey, Ketchel's defense was his offense. A murderous puncher with death at the end of each arm, Ketchel kept exploding six-inch shells in five-ounce gloves until something happened."

An apt description for sure. Ketchel always fought with murderous intentions whether it be in his unofficial 250-plus barroom fights or wading through the middleweight division until his untimely murder at the age of 24.

Ketchel was so confident of his power and conditioning that on five different occasions he fought two men on the same day. On one occasion he fought and outscored six different opponents in a six-round match taking a fresh fighter for each round. Imagine such a feat being conducted today (or even allowed by any athletic commission).

Perhaps the greatest show of his power and conditioning, if not his grit, was his taking a run at the heavyweight crown then held by the very formidable Jack Johnson. Some boxing historians tell us that the fight was a fix, a quasi-demonstration affair to drum up money for the cash-strapped champion. A set up on the order of a cake walk. Well, if this is true somebody forget to tell Stanley Ketchel. On October 16, 1909 in Colma, California, the middleweight champion met the heavyweight champion. Ketchel gave up height, reach and weight — 35 pounds to be exact (Ketchel's 170 versus Johnson's 205.) In short, Ketchel gave up every advantage there is as a fighter for a go at the heavyweight champion.

We are lucky to have an existing film of this fight and the disparity between the two is almost humorous. Ketchel looks like a child going against Johnson, a child in all things except heart. From the opening bell Ketchel wades in looking for his target. The crafty champ toys and evades round after round perhaps giving truth to the "fix" tale, but Ketchel never stopped swinging, looking for that knockout. In the 12th round Ketchel finally found his mark on the champ's jaw and dropped the bigger man. The angered champ was soon up and went after the scrappy middleweight champion and dropped him with a punch so hard that two of Ketchel's teeth were embedded in Johnson's glove.

Fix discussion aside, even in losing Ketchel demonstrated enormous strength and stamina in being able to muster the power to drop such a big, formidable man — a fighter used to being hit by the heaviest and most able fighters in the world and weathering those storms just fine. This knockdown of the champ and his long string of victories lets us know why so many boxing historians put Ketchel at the top of the middleweight pack.

Just how did Ketchel build up such extraordinary punching

power and indomitable stamina? He was noted for running a spartan training camp with a good work ethic. For the most part his training regimen mimics what you would find among many fighters of the era (and today for that matter.) Roadwork, bag work, floor work (calisthenics), sparring and so on, but there was an unusual feature of Ketchel's training that you will find with few other champions. He threw boulders.

> ... there was an unusual feature of Ketchel's training that you will find with few other champions. He threw boulders.

We'll get back to the boulder throwing in a moment, but first consider this. Combat sports, whether it be boxing, kickboxing, grappling or MMA, all rely more on rotational power than strict linear power whether that be the posterior or anterior chains. What I mean by that is strikes (punches, kicks, knees, elbows), throws, takedowns, sweeps and even cogent submission set ups utilize rotational power more than they do right angle linear efforts. Any strike worth its salt relies on rotational forces that begin at the ball of the foot and move upward through the knees, hips, waist and finally to the shoulders and arms (if the strike is a punch.) All strikes, all offensive grappling exist in this rotational domain.

What does the vast majority of our training consist of? We do push ups, squats, pull ups, dips and other bodyweight exercise, all of which are executed in up and down linear fashion. With weights we do back squats, bench presses, barbell rows, kettlebell swings and push presses, again, all exercises that exist in linear planes that do little to develop the integral rotational power of combat sports.

All of the aforementioned exercises are necessary and useful to build overall conditioning, but perhaps it was Ketchel's adherence to heavy rotational work that allowed him to be valued so highly in his own division and to be as surprising as he was when at a size disadvantage. Let's get back to Mr. Ketchel's boulder-tossing.

In addition to traditional boxing conditioning, Ketchel would spend one hour each day throwing boulders. Boulders! For one hour! He didn't simply clean, press and deadlift — he threw them. He would pick up a boulder and throw it as far as he could. Move on to the next and repeat until his hour was up. One can't help but make the assumption that this diligence and adherence to rotational specificity may very well have contributed to Ketchel's astonishing punching power and stamina. Let's consider how we might adapt Ketchel's method to today and build our own rotational power.

Many of us may not have spare boulders lying around the gym. If so, you know what to do. If not, try the following.

Stanley Ketchel rotational workout
● Grab as many slam balls or medicine balls as you can. If you have only one, make sure it's a heavy one and know that that piece of gear is going to get a lot of use.
● I use a line of four slam balls. They weigh 20, 30, 40 and 50 pounds.
● Place them all in a line behind a cone.
● Mark off 10 feet. Don't go for more than that, because you lose freshness. Ten feet is more than enough distance.

● Set your timer for 30 minutes. I do 30 minutes assuming I'm only half the man Ketchel was and that's being generous.

● Pick up the slam balls anyway you like and toss them anyway you like — push pass, swing toss, granny toss, over-head toss, your call. But mix them up making sure they cross the ten-foot line indicated by another cone.

● Walk over and send them back home over the line at the first cone.

● Since we're only playing half the time that Ketchel did, try adding a set of 10 penalty burpees for each "boulder" that falls short of the 10-foot line. I find being honest with your penalties keeps your quality of work high.

Whether this turns out to be the key to building Ketchel-esque punching power or not, there's one thing for certain, it can't hurt. Well, hurt beyond sore muscles.

16. Joe Frazier and the dark road

Roadwork. That eight-letter word is often a four-letter word to boxers in training because, to be frank, not many of us like to do it. Getting inside the gym, banging the pads, pulverizing the bags and smacking each other is way more fun than lacing up the running shoes and hitting the road. There's something about roadwork that feels so "not boxing." It's more akin to being in training for cross-country, but we can't get around it — we've got to do it. And since we have to do it, lets hit three lessons on how we can approach this gotta-do activity.

First, a sidebar regarding why boxers do roadwork in the first place instead of simply putting in more gym time. It's all about the weight. Yes, roadwork does confer some conditioning and stamina benefits, but that's not the major reason roadwork is a staple of boxing training. After all, if much of what we had to do to be better boxers was simply log more miles than the other guy, then those guys you see trotting up and down the road every day prepping for marathons are just a boxing lesson or two shy of a title shot. Anybody think that's true? Of course not.

Roadwork does indeed supply a conditioning effect, but it is not the primary reason why it has become a "must" for boxing training. There are actually other activities that will build similar (if not better) stamina, add serious strength and take far less time allowing you to get more boxing drilling in. But these activities don't cut weight like running lots and lots of miles will.

Boxers, wrestlers and MMA athletes all do roadwork because of weight classes. Weight classes allow for anywhere from a

9- to 10-pound spread for the most part and coming in at the top end of a weight class confers some serious benefits in strength and power. Mass and size make a difference, that's exactly why we have weight classes in the first place.

> "If you cheated on that in the dark of the morning, well, you're going to get found out now, under the bright lights."

If size and mass didn't matter then the talented middleweight could easily topple the journeyman heavyweight. Sometimes a good middleweight can embarrass a lackluster heavy, but all the heavyweight needs is for one of his shots to land flush and that's all she wrote.

It is for this reason that cutting weight to get to the top of a weight class where you feel you can be the strongest and baddest fighter is the ideal strategy. It's far harder to gain mass and size and still remain an effective fighter with good lungs while going up a weight class. It's far easier to cut and be the baddest lighter version of your walk-around self. I wager that if we skipped the night before weigh-in ritual and went with a step-into-the-ring natural weight system, we'd see an alteration in how roadwork is approached. But since it's not likely to happen, go ahead and lace up those shoes because you've got some miles to put in.

Back to Smokin' Joe Frazier and what he can teach us about the dark road. Since, this is a task we're not going to get around, let's make the most of it. We look to the very powerful Joe Frazier and how he approached roadwork (and all training for that matter.)

"You can map out a fight plan or a life plan, but when the action starts, it may not go the way you planned, and you're down to your reflexes — that means your [preparation]. That's where your roadwork shows. If you cheated on that in the dark of the morning, well, you're going to get found out now, under the bright lights."

Those are inspiring words that allows us to glimpse his strategic approach to roadwork. He wanted it to be tough. He wanted to do it the hardest way possible. Where others might take shortcuts, he wasn't going to do that. And because he didn't take the shortcuts, he found himself short cutting to the top of the heavyweight heap.

There's another bit of wisdom inside that quote. Recall the phrase "If you cheated on that in the dark of the morning." Frazier liked to do his roadwork early in the morning — in the dark. Not twilight, but dark. He liked the feeling of knowing that while he was putting in the time in the dark of the morning, somewhere his opponent was still snug in bed sound asleep. This knowledge conferred a bit of gritty understanding to him, that where he was willing to embrace the grind, embrace the suck, his opponent was not made of the same stuff.

Smokin' Joe wanted his training to be something that he knew his opponent would not be willing to do. Knowing that you are willing to do what the fighter in front of you will not do conveys a huge psychological advantage.

If we are to approach roadwork Joe Frazier-style, that may mean getting up early. It also means not avoiding the hills and choosing the route that assures easy ground. It may also mean leaving that iPod at home. Don't distract yourself with a travelling DJ. Frazier advises us to tap into and not necessarily overcome the resentment that we may feel by putting ourselves through this. To really embrace the suck, you've got to be hip deep in that suck, building up both the knowledge that "Yeah, I'll do this, will you?" and the grit that says "I don't need easy, I don't want easy — I train hard to fight easy." Roadwork ain't fun, but it must be done.

> "I don't need easy, I don't want easy — I train hard to fight easy."

Do we have what it takes to take Smokin' Joe's dark road?

17. Floyd Patterson's roadwork math

Floyd Patterson remains the youngest undisputed heavy-weight champion ever and the first man to regain the title after having lost it. The latter was a crushing loss to Ingemar Johansson who knocked Paterson to the canvas seven times before the referee stopped the fight in the third round. Patterson regained the title with a vicious knockout of Johansson in the fifth round of their second match. The tough Swede was out for a good five minutes before he could be guided back to his stool.

Since both men were so devastating to each other in alter-nate bouts, it only made sense to set a third fight. And a fan-tastic bout it was. Both men went down, but Patterson put Johansson away in the sixth bringing this series to a close.

There are many things we can learn from this champion. For starters, he never let his hands drop earning his defense the nickname "Peek-a-Boo" because he was always peering at opponents behind hands held good and high. He was a dis-ciplined, well-coached fighter, honed in the hands of the estimable Cus D'Amato who went on to mold Mike Tyson.

What we want to learn for today is Patterson's approach to roadwork — how he kept his mind in the game while log-ging the necessary miles to be a champion. Where Joe Frazier embraced an almost tortuous approach to roadwork, Patterson found ways to distract himself from the run itself (there were no earbuds back then to do the job). When the road grind got hard, Patterson would count his steps giving his mind something to focus on rather than the chore of the miles ahead.

We'd have an interesting animal if we combined both Smokin' Joe's and Patterson's approach.

If you are running sans earbuds as Joe Frazier would have, there is no doubt that there are some days (or dark mornings) where you will simply want to quit. It is at these times that using Patterson's distraction math may come in handy.

You can do it in many variations, a few of which are offered below:

● Count every single step: right one, left two and so on.
● Count every alternate step.
● Count steps between points. For example, counting how many steps between each mailbox along a given route.

I have found that the mix works well. When I'm feeling lean and mean on a given roadwork day, I can think and ponder and allow the head to wander where it wants while the body works. But on days where I'm feeling less than bad ass (maybe more of an irritable ass), I find that distracting myself with a little Patterson math is a nice little trick, even if it is a trick I play on myself.

18. Freddie Welsh's accelerated roadwork

Toward the end of the 19th century, in the year 1886 to be exact, a young lad christened Frederick Hall Thomas was born in Pontypridd, a village in South Wales. He would grow up to rename himself Freddie Welsh after his home country. As a matter of fact, on your next bar trivia night you can proudly exclaim that Freddie Welsh is the only champion in history whose last name was also his nationality.

Freddie did some fighting in his home country and then crossed the pond that is the Atlantic Ocean and landed in Philadelphia where he fought for a while before returning to his homeland. He would cross this formidable pond several times in a long-reaching career that saw him picking up both the British lightweight championship belt and the world lightweight title.

These zig zags across the Atlantic allowed this very clever fighter to pick up tips and tactics from both schools of boxing, British and American. He forged his own style out of this hybrid. Here's Welsh himself on his across the pond observations:

"The English boxer is too orthodox; he sticks to his style, despite all else. The American fighter conforms to the situation. If he misses a left hook, he swings right back with the right. The English boxer swings back to his position and starts again."

Freddie made this mongrel hybrid of English and American styles work wonders. Here's what another champ, the redoubtable Abe Atell, replied when asked "How do you beat Freddie Welsh?"

> He felt that a series of hard, fast sprints would do the job just as effectively, if not more effectively than lots and lots of miles.

"If you can lay a glove on that guy five times in twenty rounds, you'll get the verdict, sure! If you don't want to be made to look like a sucker, take my advice: go away and train. Train good and hard. Then sprain your ankle the night before the fight."

There are three main things that come to mind that we can learn from the great Freddie Welsh: His unerring jab, his constant and baffling movement, and his indefatigable stamina. Since we covered the first two in a previous chapter, let's concentrate on how Freddie built such endurance while skipping traditional roadwork. That get your attention, no roadwork?

Well, almost none.

Freddie Welsh skipped logging mile after endless mile and chose to use sprints to do the job. He felt that a series of hard, fast sprints would do the job just as effectively, if not more effectively than lots and lots of miles. It would take less time and allow him to put more time into boxing drills.

What Welsh stumbled onto at the beginning of the last century — that sprints can replace long, drawn out endurance work — has been borne out by contemporary exercise science. In many studies, high intensity training (HIT) performs just as well or better than traditional long slow distance (LSD) training. Freddie reasoned that boxers aren't long distance runners, but athletes who are required to give short bursts of maximum effort between brief lulls requiring less energy. Long distance running taught one to plod as opposed to bursting.

Lest anyone think that having failed to log long miles he would fade in later rounds: Welsh fought in 82 bouts lasting 20 rounds in the days of no decision. According to those in and out of the ring, he was still moving just as freshly at the end of bouts as he was at the beginning.

Let's keep in mind that Welsh did not need the one undisputed benefit of roadwork, the weight cutting effect. As a lightweight with no tendency to balloon between matches, sprints were the ideal way for him to go. If you are a disciplined fighter and stay close to your fight weight, you might be able to make use of Freddie Welsh's sprint roadwork.

Roadwork Freddie Welsh-style

For the following sample sprint workouts, there are two approaches to timing your rest/work ratio. The timed version uses a strictly timed rest between sprints. The walk-back version has you walking to rest between exercise. For example, after a 50-yard sprint, walk back to the starting line. The following sprint workouts will use a timed protocol, but in a pinch a walk-back will work.

Important: The key in all Welsh-style roadwork is intensity. You must run at your maximum speed for the given distance. Holding back is sandbagging and short circuiting the point of using sprints as a viable roadwork shortcut. Perform diligently with maximum intensity. If you realize you are holding back, either step it up or go back to long, hard miles.

Day 1
- Sprint 50 yards
- Rest 30 seconds
- x 12 (repeat 12 times)

Day 2
- Sprint 100 yards
- Rest 45 seconds
- x 12

Day 3
- Sprint 400 yards
- Rest 1 minute
- x 6

Day 4
- Repeat Day 1

Day 5
- Sprint 800 yards
- Rest 2 minutes
- x 2

Day 6
- Repeat Day 2

Day 7
- Sprint 1 mile
- Rest 5 minutes
- Then Sprint 50 yards
- Rest 30 seconds
- x 5

Day 8
- Sprint backwards 50 yards
- Rest 30 seconds
- x 12

Day 9
- Sprint 800 yards
- Rest 90 seconds
- x 4

Day 10
- Repeat Day 1

Day 11
- Sprint 1/2 mile
- Rest 2 minutes
- x 3

Day 12
- Repeat Day 2

Lucky Day 13
- Sprint 50 yards
- Rest 30 seconds
- Sprint 100 Yards
- Rest 45 seconds
- Sprint 200 yards
- Rest 1 minute
- Sprint 1/2 mile
- Rest 3 minutes
- Sprint 1 mile

Once you have moved through this cycle, go back to Day 1 and walk yourself back through the sequence. If you've been timing your sprints from cycle to cycle you should be able to chart major improvement Freddie Welsh-style.

19. Sonny Liston's secret to taking a punch

Take a look at any photo or film of Sonny Liston and you will see one powerful and imposing figure. He stood 6-foot, 1-inch and weighed around 218 pounds. None of it soft. His fists were 15 inches in circumference. This is rumored to be greater than those of the far larger champs, Jess Willard and Primo Carnera. Both of those guys stood over six and a half feet.

What added to Liston's imposing frame was a neck that measured 17 1/2 inches in circumference. That neck was no accident. Liston worked at developing it to better absorb punches. He figured (rightly) that a strong neck was better able to react to and absorb blows that penetrated his defense.

Many modern boxers do little to no neck work. If they do it at all, it's simply done with a head strap that allows the boxer to attach weight and work some resistance reps. This was not Liston's way. So how did he build such a massive neck and trapezius foundation without weights?

Building a Liston-like, shock absorber neck
He would stand on his head. That's it. If the accounts are to be believed, he would stand on his head for an hour or two while listening to his favorite song "Night Train."

Now perhaps we don't have hours to spare standing on our heads, but we can take this tip from Liston and add similar knowledge from how wrestler's build their necks so that we can gain similar shock-absorbing support.

Neck bridge

● Lie on the floor with the back of your head on the floor.
● Rock up onto the top of your head supporting yourself only with your feet and head.
● Rock a little to the left and right.
● Rock a little back and forth.
● Strive to hold and rock in this position initially for only a minute. Eventually work to a total of five minutes and you'll build some respectable neck strength.

Front neck bridge

● This time support yourself on your head and toes while facing downward.
● Run the same slow rock forward and back.
● Then side to side.
● Use the same protocol of one minute initially and build to a continuous five minutes.

Side-to-side work

The following resistance exercise will help build resilience to a punch that catches you at the hook angle.

● Turn your face to the left.
● Place your right palm on the right side of your face.
● Turn your head slowly all the way to the right while applying resistance with your right hand the entire way.
● Fight the turn in this manner for 20-30 reps.
● Then return the favor on the other side.

This regimen of neck work followed 3-4 days per week will build a respectable Liston-esque neck while saving us hours of headstand time. By the way, bonus points if you throw on a copy of "Night Train" while you work.

Neck bridge

Front neck bridge

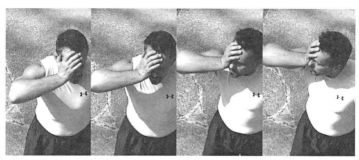

Side-to-side resistance exercise

Historical artifacts

Time to close it out with a couple of lessons in illegal tactics. These are no longer kosher by modern boxing standards, although some are OK in MMA. I offer them as a sort of fun, adjunct training exercise. A nice way to play historical re-enactor without having to dress up in blue or gray.

BAT. NELSON

20. Battling Nelson and the scissors punch

Warning: This lesson from the masters is a no-go in today's boxing and MMA rules, but it still holds value for self-defense. It's insane to think that such tactics were at one time hunkydory.

Let's spend a little time with a man whose parents seemed to have had some idea of what they were bringing forth when they christened him Oscar Matthew Battling Nelson. While raised in the United States, Nelson was born in Copenhagen, Denmark which led to another nickname, "The Durable Dane." And durable he was.

Nelson was never a noted stylist, he was as far from pretty as one can get. But he was old school tough. He would emerge from his corner with his arms crossed in front of him and start throwing with wild abandon, always swinging

> As fearsome as he was, no one mistook what he did inside the ring for anything resembling "the sweet science."

for the fences. Nelson could be the poster boy for the "I'll take three of his to give one of mine" school of fighting. Notice I said fighting and not boxing. As fearsome as he was, no one mistook what he did inside the ring for anything resembling "the sweet science."

Battling Nelson (often shortened to simply Bat), went after an opponent and kept coming no matter what the consequences. He fought two 40-round fights, both among the 10 longest bouts of the 20th century. In one of those bouts, in 1902 versus Christy Williams, there were a total of 49 knockdowns — the most in boxing history. Bat was down seven times, Williams 42 (which establishes Williams as being mighty durable himself).

Our Durable Dane once broke his left arm in the middle rounds of a 15-rounder, but soldiered on, explaining at the end of the fight, "It made me somewhat cautious and kept me winning by a knockout."

There is no doubt that Battling Nelson was one of the most ferocious fighters to ever step into the ring, but this already mentioned lack of finesse would seem to preclude him from teaching 21st century fighters anything about the sweet science. After all, physical hardihood and sheer pluck is hard to drill.

As you might have guessed, Nelson was not the cleanest of fighters, his inside work was exceptionally savage. Jack London, the noted author of such classics as "The Call of the Wild" and "The Sea Wolf," was also an avid boxing fan (did a bit of boxing himself) and often reported on major fights for newspapers. London, not a big fan of the Dane's style, dubbed him, "The Abysmal Brute."

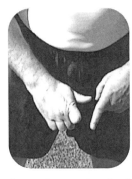 One of Bat's quasi-legal tactics was dubbed the "scissors" punch. In the era of skintight gloves, Nelson would fire a lead hook to the liver with his thumb and index finger extended in scissors fashion. This additional bit of pin-point penetration when the body is used to percussive blows is a bit more disconcerting than you would think. It has not been determined whether Nelson would deliver the scissors punch with his hook hand palm facing down or up, but experimentation has revealed, at least for me, that the palm-down version allows for better liver penetration.

Before you go smacking the bag or pads with this bit of nastiness, allow me to say that my experimentation has also revealed that my hands are not as durable as the Durable Dane's. That is, I find it's mighty easy to jam my thumb and particularly my index finger. But the following variation/adaptation seems to work nicely for those with anything less than Battling Nelson's adamantine skeleton. I have dubbed it the Nelson dig.

Nelson dig

● Fire your lead hook to the liver, but ...
● As it travels, turn the hand palm down.
● Extend the thumb, but not completely, while giving a bit of support with the second knuckle of the index finger.

Once you find the correct thumb and forefinger bolstering position, this blow can be delivered with some surprising speed and power, although it doesn't need a lot of push behind it. That penetrating shot to the liver is very unsettling.

Again, this tactic is for the street or historical recreation purposes.

21. Negative lesson from a nonchamp

Jack Dempsey was a legend.

No, not the brawling heavyweight also known as the Manassa Mauler (a legend if there ever was one). That Jack Dempsey was actually named William Harrison Dempsey. Some say he picked up the nickname, "Jack," as a boy. Others say he adopted it because of a legendary fighter that preceded him, also called Jack Dempsey. The earlier Dempsey is the one I want to talk about.

This Jack Dempsey wasn't named Jack Dempsey either. He was born John Kelly in Country Kildare, Ireland in 1862. Dempsey was his stepfather's surname. He adopted it and used it when he traveled as part of a wrestling duo with his brother. Unsurprisingly, they called themselves The Dempsey Brothers.

Note: At the turn of the last century there were a breed of fighters called combination men. These were athletes who competed in both boxing and wrestling, sometimes in mixed matches of the twin sports on the same card. These athletes, these combination men with our Jack Dempsey among them, were the original mixed martial artists of the modern era. There is a mighty interesting story here to be told and many lessons to learn from these combination men, but we'll leave that for another day.

So, we've got two excellent fighters named Jack Dempsey. As stated, the later and bigger man went by the ring name Manassa Mauler (Manassa was his Colorado hometown). This Dempsey was brutal, vicious and relentless just like his moniker suggested. Our earlier Jack Dempsey was nicknamed the "Nonpareil" which is a dandy bit of French that translates to having no match, unequaled, unrivaled and, to many eyes of the time, unbeatable. In his early career, that unbeatable estimation looked to be almost true. Out of his first 65 bouts he was only "beaten" three times. Once by George LaBlanche and twice by Billy Baker.

Baker must have been good, right? Not quite. Notice that when I said the Nonpareil was beaten I placed that word in scare quotes. There is good authority that has the two bouts with Baker as being fixes, so we can scrub those two "losses" from the record. But the loss to George LaBlanche, well, LaBlanche not only beat him, he poleaxed him, dropping him to the canvas like so much cordwood.

We must assume that George "The Marine" La Blanche was pretty damn good, right? I mean he did not only beat the unbeatable, he knocked him cold. Let's look at that fight and how the unbeatable was beaten. They faced each other in August of 1889, and the Nonpareil appeared to be just that. For the first 31 rounds he used his enviable speed and quick combinations to keep The Marine lit up.

Then in the 32nd round LaBlanche hit the unbeatable with an uncommon punch that was used sparingly in pugilism's early days and rarely in the gloved era. What was this punch?

Pivot punch

This punch is essentially a spinning, straight-arm blow that uses the inertial forces of centrifugal energy to slam this bad boy home, and LaBlanche slammed it home hard. Although not strictly prohibited by the Marquis of Queensbury rules, LaBlanche was still disqualified, and this loss for the Nonpareil was not so much a loss as a bit of a puzzle. I mean, here we have one of the best of the early era falling and falling hard from what is a mighty risky blind blow.

For a bit of historical fun, let's reconstruct this now illegal blow that dropped a champ. Hey, MMA cadre — you can still throw this one to your heart's content.

Blind blow

This is a blind blow and a sacrifice punch. That is, one that calls for turning your back to your opponent and betting all your chips on you being able to hit a moving target. With that caveat in mind, you decide just how much time you want to devote to this tactic.

Pivot punch mechanics

● From your boxing stance, step the lead toes across to be on a single line with the toes of the rear foot.

● Pivot on the balls of your feet until you are facing 180 degrees in the opposite direction.

● Turn your head to look back at your opponent over your rear shoulder.

● Uncoil the rear arm and swing, striking your target with the bottom of your fist.

The above steps are meant to be hit in rapid succession to reduce back-to-opponent time and to make the most of the centrifugal inertia. With practice the step across almost becomes a bit of a short leap into position.

"Missed" hook

● You can hide this one inside of a combination.

● Let's throw a jab/cross and then a lead hook ...

● But allow your lead hook to fall short and sweep past its "target"...

● While stepping the lead foot into position to execute the pivot punch.

True missed hook

● You can also train yourself to throw with an actual miss of the lead hook.

● To train this it is helpful to have a good pad feeder set you up for combinations of jab/cross/lead hook.

● Allow your feeder to present all three targets, but ...

● Occasionally have them pull the pad for the lead hook.

● When you feel the miss, launch directly into your pivot punch set up.

Defensive pivot punch versus a loss of position

Occasionally you will encounter a speed demon whose footwork gets them to your back. You can either wheel back into position or fire the pivot from this quasi set up.

● Have your feeder work a set root combination.
● Occasionally they will speed rush to your outside and back.
● Immediately turn and fire the pivot punch from your loss-of-position stance.

Duelist jab

A duelist jab steals a bit of footwork from old west gun-fighters. To fire a high-caliber firearm with a single hand it was necessary to provide skeletal support throughout the entire body. Attempting to hold the heavy weapon and its recoil still by force of your lead shoulder and chest muscles alone was very difficult. The duelist stance had the shooter stepping the lead toes in line with the rear toes and extending the weapon hand forward from this more stable position.

● To throw the duelist jab, step the lead toes in line with the rear toes.

● As soon as the lead toes hit position, fire the jab straight from the shoulder along with a bit of upright and inward hip pop.

● This hip pop provides what little power the duelist jab has.

Duelist jab to pivot punch

Let's now put this into a combination sequence to mask our intentions.

- Throw a standard jab.
- Throw another to set a precedent.
- Now, throw your duelist jab.
- Continue from your duelist jab stance into a pivot punch spin.

Since the pivot always leaves you with your back to your opponent, it is wise to end a pivot with a step away.

Pivot punch step away

● Upon the back-hand blow landing ...

● Step the lead foot (the one closest to your opponent) forward, toward your chest and away from your opponent as if sprinting.

● Take a step or two away to get some distance and safely turn back to your opponent.

Again, illegal in contemporary boxing and questionable even in the old days, but completely free to use in MMA. If anything it's a historical blast to work what dropped a dominant fighter like a sack of potatoes.

Calling it a day for now

I could go on and on with more tips, tactics, tricks (both of the dirty and not-so-dirty variety), strategy, and conditioning secrets of the masters, but we've got to call it a day some-where. It seems a shame because we are just scratching the surface. These giants have lessons for us, and I look forward to relating more of them in the future.

One last thing, hold up your hand. Make a fist. Look at that fist. This book and the lessons within are now the brains to go into that fist. Now, go train!

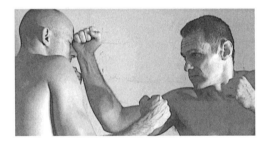

Bibliography
Historical information was largely gleaned from these sources:

Edwards, Billy. Legendary Boxers of the Golden Age. London: Southwater Publishing, 2013.

Fleischer, Nate and Andre, Sam. An Illustrated History of Boxing. Secaucus, New Jersey: Carol Publishing Group, 1997.

Heller, Peter. "In This Corner ...!": 42 World Champions Tell Their Stories. New York, New York: Da Capo Press, 1994.

Roberts, James B. and Skutt, Alexander G. The Boxing Register. Ithaca, New York: McBooks Press, Inc., 2011.

Silver, Mike. The Arc of Boxing. Jefferson, North Carolina: McFarland & Company, Inc., 2008.

Sugar, Bert Randolph. Boxing's Greatest Fighters. Guilford, Connecticut: The Lyons Press, 2006.

Weston, Stanley and Farhood, Steven. The Ring: Boxing The 20th Century. New York: BDD Illustrated Books, 1993.

YouTube

How I analyzed the champs for this book
I read the historical sources and made notes of folks or tactics I wanted to look into deeper. Then I simply dialed up the fighter on YouTube and watched every match available and made copious notes.

Then I went to the gym to seat the skills. Some took quite a bit of work! Eder Jofre's crunch hook comes to mind. That took some experimentation to figure out how he was creating power with that rear leg dig.

Mark Hatmaker

Tommy Gibbons

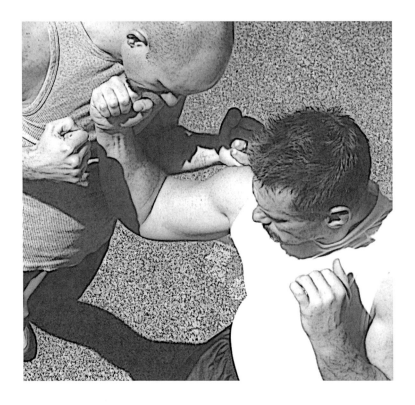

Index

Joe Louis and Max Schmeling

Mark Hatmaker is the bestselling author of the *No Holds Barred Fighting Series*, the *MMA Mastery Series*, *No Second Chance* and *Boxing Mastery*. He also has produced more than 40 instructional videos. His resume includes extensive experience in the combat arts including boxing, wrestling, Jiu-jitsu and Muay Thai.

He is a highly regarded coach of professional and amateur fighters, law enforcement officials and security personnel. Hatmaker founded Extreme Self Protection (ESP), a research body that compiles, analyzes and teaches the most effective Western combat methods known. ESP holds numerous seminars throughout the country each year including the prestigious Karate College/Martial Arts Universities in Radford, Virginia. He lives in Knoxville, Tennessee.

www.extremeselfprotection.com

Tracks Publishing
Ventura, California